dvance Praise for *Firescaping*

f you want to be more responsible for your home's fire safety, follow these guidelines."
-Dick Hayes, Deputy Chief, Public Education, California Department of Forestry and Fire Protection

'ery well done ... with loads of useful information."
-Scott Alber, Fire Marshal, Marin County

'hould be the required text for every firefighter, homeowner, and landscape architect where even a remote ·ance of fire may occur."
-Bob Tanem, America's Happy Gardener, and garden radio host on KSFO

'ery comprehensive and filled with useful information."
-Ken Churches, County Director, University of California Cooperative Extension

'elpful examples of various tools to design and maintain landscapes that protect homes from this ever- ·esent hazard."
-Darren Haver, South Coast Research and Extension Center, University of California Cooperative Ex- nsion

...contains a wealth of information for anyone serious about community wildfire protection and proper 'getation management ... an excellent tool for teaching forestry, silviculture, and horticulture students out fire-related topics."
-David R. Caine, Fire Commissioner, Lake Arrowhead Fire District, and representative for Senator Jim rulte, Governor's Blue Ribbon Fire Commission 2004

'oug Kent not only points out the problems and suggests solutions, but he offers the aesthetic advice of garden designer and then backs that up with the growing knowledge of a gardener."
-Robert Smaus, author of *Answers for California Gardeners* and *52 Weeks in the California Garden*

D1122389

FIRESCAPING

FIRESCAPING

Creating fire-resistant landscapes, gardens, and properties in California's diverse environments

 **WILDERNESS PRESS** · BERKELEY, CA

Firescaping: Creating fire-resistant landscapes, gardens, and properties in California's diverse environments

1st EDITION May 2005

Front cover illustration copyright © 2005 by Rodica Prato
Interior illustrations by Richard Kent, Edward Thishburn, and Douglas Kent
Interior photos, except where noted, by Douglas Kent and Jim Evans
Chapter opening photos copyright © 2005 by Brian Kemble

Cover design: Hayden Foell
Book design: Hayden Foell
Book editors: Ellen Cavalli and Eva Dienel

ISBN: 0-89997-360-4
UPC 7-19609-97360-7

Manufactured in the United States of America

Published by: **Wilderness Press**
1200 5th Street
Berkeley, CA 94710
(800) 443-7227; FAX (510) 558-1696
info@wildernesspress.com
www.wildernesspress.com

Visit our website for a complete listing of our books and for ordering information.

NOTICE: Although Wilderness Press and the author have made every attempt to ensure that the information in this book is accurate at press time, they are not responsible for any loss, damage, injury, or inconvenience that may occur to anyone while using this book. Following the advice in this book does not guarantee protection against fire risk. You are responsible for your own safety, as well as the safety of your home, property, and belongings.

Library of Congress Cataloging-in-Publication Data

Kent, Douglas (Douglas K.)
   Firescaping : creating fire-resistant landscapes, gardens, and properties in California's diverse environments / Douglas Kent.-- 1st ed.
      p. cm.
   Includes bibliographical references (p.   ) and index.
   ISBN 0-89997-360-4 (pbk.)
   1. Firescaping--California. I. Title.

SB475.9.F57K46 2005
635.9'5--dc22
                                        2004030064

Contents

Introduction

In 1995, my beat usually didn't put me in such distressing situations. But there I was, getting off a bus after visiting the front lines of a forest fire ravaging Inverness and the Point Reyes area of west Marin County. The fire official dropped all the journalists off on a street that had suffered considerable damage—nearly three out of four houses had been destroyed. Minutes later, two more buses roared up with the residents of the street. What followed was gut-wrenchingly sad.

As the residents slowly discovered the fate of their homes, I saw astonishment, disbelief, and pain. An older couple sat on a charred pine, starring at the remains of their home, a chimney and metal file cabinet. The couple would not talk or look at anybody. I heard a middle-aged women hollering for two cats. When I left two hours later, she was still calling for them. I joined a young man while he meekly joked about his smoldering car, his only real asset.

For a garden writer, the scene was tough. From silence and sobs, to denial and anguish, the range of emotion was deafening. Their problems plagued my thoughts for days. Where would they spend the night? How would they make a living? What does loss of that magnitude feel like?

Just eight years later, I witnessed loss of an even greater magnitude. This time it was the Cedar fire, which ripped through more than 273,000 acres in and around San Diego in a span of six-and-a-half days. The fire left 14 people dead and 2,820 homes destroyed. By the end of the year, 2003 held the record for the state's most destructive fire season in history. All told, fires were responsible for 22 deaths and more than 5,000 lost structures. Even still, Cedar was not the worst fire in California's history. In 1991, the Oakland/Berkeley Tunnel fire burned 1,600 acres, and consumed 25 lives and 2,900 structures—all

in just 10 hours. The terrorizing ferocity of that fire still haunts the area.

Since 1990, 53 lives and more than 11,000 structures in California have been lost to wildfires. During that same period, Californians have seen 14 of the state's worst fires, including the five most destructive. These escalating episodes of disaster are costly. The state has estimated that it will cost nearly $1.3 billion dollars a year to fight wildfires and provide disaster relief. Adjusted for inflation, the Tunnel fire cost insurers $2.2 billion, and the fires of 2003 are expected surpass that number. But not all the costs are as visible: Fires lead to a variety of respiratory health problems, erosion and water-quality issues that persist for years, and high costs for public and private institutions alike.

Experts say that the worst is yet to come. According to the California Department of Forestry and Fire Protection (CDF), all of California's wild lands will burn at some point. The CDF predicts that fires of the future will be larger, more intense, and more damaging than ever before. This is because California today faces a swelling population, a scarcity of flat land, and overgrown landscapes.

California's population has leaped since 1900, when only 1.4 million people lived in the state. Today, California has more than 35 million residents, and the population is expected to reach 40 million by 2012. Almost every county can expect more people, but according to the state Department of Finance, the largest population growth will take place in San Joaquin, Merced, Riverside, Placer, and Madera counties—most of which climb up the flammable foothills of the Sierra Nevada's western flank. Already, nearly one in four Californians live in fire country. Some reside in old towns surrounded by flammable landscaping; others live off small, winding roads. Most of these people and their communities are not taking all of the steps necessary to protect themselves.

It doesn't have to be like this. After every fire, some homes survive in neighborhoods that have been engulfed by flames. Along with the devastation at the site of the 1995 fire in Marin County, I saw glimmers of hope: Homes still standing amid tombs of chimneys and large piles of twisted debris. Their walls were a sticky grayish black, their corners or overhangs were licked and charred, but the homes had survived. Surveying the site, I began to wonder why the fire spared some homes and not others. Living in a similar environment, I wondered if I could do anything to save my home from the destructive power of fire.

After years of work, I can now answer that question firmly: Yes—there are many steps I can take to reduce the risk of losing my home. People and homes can survive fires. The greatest impact residents can have in their community is to create their own fire-protected property. One protected property lowers the risk of neighboring properties, and when an entire neighborhood is protected, the risk is lower still for surrounding communities.

At the center of this protection is a firescaped garden. Firescaping is not a look or style, but a method of protecting your property from fire danger. There are three goals for firescaping: Plants should be kept healthy, debris should be picked up, and ample space should be cleared between clusters of plants.

This book will help you lower the risk of fire damage to your home and community by teaching you how keep your property healthy, clean, and clear. The first part of this book is devoted to the foundation of firescaping: the history of fire in California, how to assess your own property, and the theory behind the design of an effectively firescaped garden. Chapters 5 through 9 provide the tools for action, with lessons on how to reclaim a landscape, which plants are most appropriate to use, and how to maintain a landscape that is as good for security as it is for beauty. The last chapter outlines the measures needed to minimize erosion after a fire passes.

As you will read in the Perspectives section in every chapter, many residents have had multiple brushes with fire. I have been on the front lines of three fires—a mild claim to many. I have also helped my parents evacuate, which was a spooky experience for everyone in their neighborhood. But watching the residents of west Marin return home in 1995 has been the most scarring. No one should have to endure that type of pain.

I hope this book will help you prepare your home and property so that fire is not welcome in your neighborhood. If more people use the tools for firescaping described in this book, we just might see less damage to the property and communities of our state. But we need get out there and start now. Fire doesn't sit patiently in committee and board meetings. Fire roams California's landscapes, which is where our efforts should be.

My sleeves are rolled up. I hope you are ready, too.

Chapter 1

Fire in California

When it comes to fire, California is unlike any other state: It is the most flammable, the most dangerous, and its fire season lasts nearly eight months. Fires have been racing across our landscape for millions of years, and nothing has changed today. Each year, modern Californians can expect about 6,300 fires, which, based on averages taken between 1999 and 2003, will burn approximately 193,000 acres, 1,530 structures, and will take five lives.

The state is this way due to a unique combination of climate, terrain, location, and history. California is comfortably situated on the globe in a region close to the sea, in a moderate latitude, with a mountainous terrain—all of which create favorable conditions for fire. The reason it never rains on the Rose Parade also explains why our fire season is so long: A high-pressure system that lingers off the coast pushes storms up and away from the state.

While natural forces determined the condition of fire in California for millions of years, people began to have an effect on fire in this region beginning about 12,000 years ago. At that time, the native people who settled the landscape quickly discovered that fire could be used as a tool, and they regularly set the land ablaze. The European adventurers and entrepreneurs who arrived about 500 years ago also learned to live with fire, building structures and compounds that allowed fires to burn around them. By the mid-1800s, however, Californians' attitude about fire changed: Fire was seen as a threat to their resources and land, and they put their efforts into fighting it.

After more than 150 years, that outlook remains largely the same. As a result, California's mature landscapes have been without fire for decades. We are also in the midst of a climatic warming trend. Hotter days and massive fuel loads is a dangerous mix, and because of this, the intensity of future fires is expected to grow.

This chapter describes the condition of fire in California, and how the Golden State has become the most flammable state in the country. It explains the factors that influence fire frequency and intensity, and it examines the many relationships that humans have had with fire, beginning with the native Californians and ending with the current residents. Finally, this chapter describes modern fire-management policy, which is gradually shifting in focus from prevention to protection. In the end, this confirms that adapting our communities to fire is smarter than trying to fight it.

California's 10 Most Destructive Fires

1991: Oakland/Berkeley Tunnel Fire—25 lives and 2,900 structures lost

2003: San Diego Cedar Fire—14 lives and 2,820 structures lost

2003: San Bernardino—6 lives and 1,003 structures lost

1999: Shasta—1 life and 954 structures lost

1990: Santa Barbara—1 life and 641 structures lost

1992: Shasta—636 structures lost

1923: City of Berkeley—584 structures lost

1961: Los Angeles—484 structures lost

1993: Laguna Beach—441 structures lost

2003: San Diego—2 lives and 415 structures lost

Source: California Department of Forestry and Fire Protection

Perspectives: Robert Smaus, Retired Garden Editor, *Los Angeles Times*

There's no sense putting our heads down a hole, ostrichlike. California is going to burn, or at least the wild portions of it—every square inch, sooner or later. Historically, flames have danced across the chaparral and sage, raced though grasslands, and cleansed oak and conifer forests. It's a fire ecology. Things depend on it. Bugs won't stop their rampage till they're toast. There are plants that can't propagate without fire, and trees that can't compete without its help. In this dry state, dead and cast-off limbs and leaves would decay very slowly if fire didn't do the occasional recycling and cleanup.

When we build in or up against wildlands, we are in fire's path. But there are things we can do to slow or even stop its onrush. We can site the house so it doesn't end up on top of a chimney of flame. We can make defensible areas that put more than an arm's length between flames and family. There are plants that aren't as flammable, and maintenance techniques that make them even less so. There are things you can do to make it easier and safer for firefighters to come to your aid.

Perhaps someday, sensible planning will separate wild plants that need to burn from homes and gardens that don't, and shouldn't. But in the meantime, it's up to individual gardeners to draw the line that fire dare not cross. In big enough blazes, driven by screaming wind, nothing will stop flames or flying embers except for carefully designed and maintained structures, and gardens will buy time for an orderly escape. When you return, there just might be something still standing. It happens all the time, and one can usually see, even on the TV, things that saved a house here or a garden there.

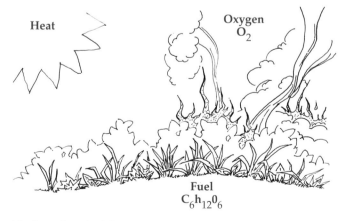

Fire's recipe: fuel, heat and oxygen

The Hot State

What makes California such a hot state? Fire needs only three elements to exist—oxygen, fuel, and heat—and California possesses all of these key ingredients in abundance. The single greatest contributing factor to the accumulation of fuel and heat is the climate.

Climate

California's climate creates the conditions for frequent fires. The climate is commonly considered Mediterranean, which is characterized by wet, moderate winters and dry, hot summers. Second to the tropics, Mediterranean climates have one of the longest growing seasons, which also means that they can create a lot of plant fuels. Parts of Africa, Asia, Australia, and South America that share our climate also share our problems with fire. The other climate types found in California—most notably the temperate regions in the north, the alpine regions in the mountains, and the desert regions in the east/southeast—are also fire prone, but not to the same degree as the milder climate regions.

Rainfall influences the amount of fuels that can grow on a landscape; consequently, the plant communities in California vary as much as the annual rainfall. With up to 60 inches of rain falling each year in the mountains, and fewer than 8 inches in the deserts, there's plenty of moisture to create fuel, but not always enough to keep it moist.

During the weeks after the last spring rain, plants continue to pull moisture from the ground. But plants dry as the soil does. In periods of drought, annuals are usually the first to wither and die, followed by perennials and shrubs, and eventually trees. Since the amount of heat required to ignite a plant is related to its moisture content, the drier the plant, the easier it is to ignite. Although wildfires are less frequent in spring, they can follow dry winters.

Along with the relatively mild winters and long summers, California possesses two quirky climatic phenomena: the Pacific high and foehn winds. The Pacific high is the name for a high-pressure weather system that hangs off our coast for most of the year. This high is responsible for our prevailing westerlies and beautiful days. However, this pressure system will sometimes weaken, and if it does so when a high-pressure system is sitting over the Great Basin, the conditions are perfect for foehn winds (such as the Santa Anas).

Foehn winds are the driving forces behind the largest conflagrations in the state. Starting from the east and blowing toward the ocean, the moisture is sucked out of these winds as they are shot up and around the mountain ranges. Humidity can drop as low as 7 percent and wind speeds can climb to 100 miles per hour. Almost any type of fire started in these winds becomes uncontrollable.

Plants

It is a widespread myth that plants influence the frequency of fire in California. In fact, the climate has a much greater influence. An especially dry pine forest is just as ignitable as a dry chaparral and grass landscape—the climate creates the conditions for all. This also means that, even given the large differences in vegetation, no part of the state is more or less immune to fire. Of the state's top 10 fires based on structure loss, six have occurred in southern California and four have happened in northern California.

When it comes to fire intensity, however, plants do have a large impact: The amount of burning vegetation determines a fire's intensity. A grassy landscape and a forested landscape represent the two extremes in danger. While a grass fire moves fast, it burns at lower temperatures, for short periods, and it may not produce long flames. On the other hand, a forest fire can burn in excess of 2,000°F, it can burn and smolder for weeks (sometimes months), and it can produce flame lengths in excess of 100 feet. The amount of heat a landscape produces when inflamed, and the length of time it keeps the fire going, are two factors that greatly affect a structure's chances of survival—and heat and duration are dictated by the amount of vegetation in a landscape. California's fire-prone landscapes can be divided into five broad groups, based on the amount of fuel they possess. These fuel categories, and their relationship with fire, are described below:

- **Savannah:** Dominated by grasses and also called grasslands and prairie, these landscapes occupy some of the hottest areas in California. Fire preserves the savannah and it may succumb to scrub without it. A fire spreads rapidly in a savannah because of wafer-thin fuels, but it is also easier extinguish because it has the least amount of fuels.

- **Scrub:** These landscapes have a combination of grasses and perennials and, like savannah, are found in some of the driest environments in the state: on the lower, eastern side of the Sierra and south-facing slopes of coastal mountains. Scrub includes plants like coyotebrush, sages, and, in the moister regions, blackberries and yerba buena. Many plants in this community live only seven to 15 years, and regular fires help their regeneration.

- **Chaparral:** These highly adapted fire communities are characterized by woody shrubs such as chamise, coffeeberry, manzanita, and toyon. Chaparral covers about 8 percent of the state and is found in the arid portions of the mountains with poor soils. The plants in this community have two chief adaptations to fire: the ability to resprout and/or the ability to produce seeds stimulated by fire—both of which ensure their succession.

- **Mixed evergreen forest:** Found throughout the cooler sides and cracks of our mountains, these communities have a combination of broadleaf and conifer shrubs and trees. The plants have enormous variation and include madrone, tanbark oak, live oak, bay, Douglas fir, black oak, ponderosa pine, and incense cedar. There is enough moisture in these communities to support a lot of vegetation, and without regular fires these forests become impassible and explosive.

- **Conifer forests:** Fir, pine, redwood, or sequoia dominate these landscapes. Tree rings from the giant sequoias in Mariposa Grove (Mariposa County) suggest that a fire ran through the grove every seven to eight years between 1760 and 1900. Most of these fires had human origins, but fires started by lightning are not uncommon in conifer forests.

Humans: The Fire Species

The West Coast's early inhabitants neither feared nor fought fire. For possibly as long as 12,000 years, many of the indigenous people regularly and intentionally set California's highly ignitable land ablaze. They burned the landscape to make traveling easier; to encourage the spread of preferred grasses, herbs, and animals; and to drive insects and game into collection areas. Occasionally, they started fires by accident; at other times, lightning torched the earth. They also understood how to use backfire to protect their homes when a blaze went out of control.

Evolution by Fire

For centuries, fire has played a dominant role in determining the character of California's landscape, and because of that, the relationship between fire and California's many different plant communities is complex. The evolution of these communities is as much tied to fire as it is to the area's specific environment.

In particular, the frequency of fire over a large span of time influences a plant community's adaptations to fire. And the more fires in a region, the more specialized plants' adaptations become.

Many California-native plants possess adaptations that help them survive and/or reproduce after a fire passes. These adaptations include thick seed coats, the ability to resprout if injured, heat-resistant bark, heat-stimulated cones, and accelerated maturity. Plants such as ceanothus, chamise, manzanita, and many annuals, such as legumes, have adapted to centuries of fire, which greatly enhances regeneration. They produce seeds with unusually thick coats that prevent seeds from drying. These coats ensure the seed a long life in the soil and require either a fire or prolonged rain to stimulate germination. Laurel sumac, toyon, oak, manzanita, and many other shrubs resprout from their injured stumps when burned to the ground, sometimes weeks after a fire. Some of the fleshier plants, like ferns and grasses, possess perennial roots that enable them to resprout after a fire.

Furthermore, many plants, such as some sages and ceanothus, have relatively short life spans, between 15 and 25 years. These shrubs almost ensure a fire on a regular basis by providing dead plant material that is easy to ignite, which, in turn, ensures their succession.

The plant communities in California's moist and cool areas, such as the mixed evergreen forests, have adapted to a lower frequency of fire. Although a lot of the shrubs found in these vast plant communities will resprout after a fire, not all possess as many adaptations as their chaparral counterparts. However, there is a correlation between a native plant's life expectancy and its resistance to fire—the longer the life span, the greater the resistance.

The redwood, one of California's longest-living trees, has many apparent adaptations to fire. Heat-resistant bark and a robust resprouting ability, both from below its crown and along its trunk, make a mature redwood highly resistant to fire. Along with an enormous amount of duff (litter), redwoods produce a lot of seed. When a fire eventually burns a redwood forest, it removes the less resistant trees and clears the ground of duff. The few surviving seeds get the benefit of full soil contact, reduced competition, and plenty of nutrients. In that way, fire aids a redwood's chances of reproduction.

Although plants such as redwood, manzanita, and many others have highly specialized adaptations that allow them to benefit from fire, no one particular plant is dependent upon fire. A prolonged and wet winter can stimulate seeds with thick seed coats. The resprouting ability of certain plants is useful when these plants are eaten, damaged, or cut.

If any type of dependence exists, it is with the plant communities and not the individual plants. Fire is needed for health and stability; it has been a part of these plant communities for thousands of years. The lack of regular fire, due to today's highly successful fire-suppression policies, has dramatically changed the nature of many native plant communities.

This approach toward fire had a profound effect on the landscape. Regular fires reduced the amount of combustible plant fuels. The burns created large, open, parklike spaces. They created a patchwork of different plant communities, which varied in density and age. The natives' use of fire also favored particular plants and animals. After the land burned, deer and large scavengers thrived because of the abundance of nutrient-rich grasses and smaller dead animals. It was unusual for a lot of dead plant fuel to accumulate. The wildfires of the past were rarely ever as severe as the ones we experience today.

New Settlers, New Approaches to Fire

In 1542, California's first European explorer, Juan Rodríguez Cabrillo, sailed into San Pedro harbor and named it the Bay of Smokes. In 1579, the notorious English sailor Sir Francis Drake sailed out of a small bay in central Oregon that he called the Bay of Fires. In 1769, Spain sent missionaries into California, and on their historical trip up the coast, Franciscan monks were stopped by fire many times.

The missions' architecture demonstrates the monks' understanding of fire, for they built structures that allowed fire to burn around them. Thick adobe walls with small windows, tile roofs, cleared landscapes, and even the trees, such as olives, helped the compounds survive. However, unlike the natives, they did not employ fire as a tool; they considered that to be a primitive use of the landscape.

The mission era came to an end in 1822, when Mexico assumed control of the state. During this time, American fur traders from the East Coast began sailing to the West in increasing numbers, and they eventually settled here. In 1848, after a brief uprising, California was ceded to the United States. The same year, John Sutter discovered gold while building his mill, and American prospectors flooded the state and laid the foundations for modern-day California.

Along with a new regime, the Americans brought a completely different idea of land management. Landowners, ranchers, miners, loggers, fishermen, and trappers saw the landscape as a commodity and fire as a threat to their livelihoods. Unfortunately, the new settlers knew little about the frequency of wildfires, and most of the early mining and logging towns were destroyed several times over. Fire-suppression efforts began in earnest in the mid-1800s, and in 1944, the National Forest Service created the Smokey Bear campaign to promote fire awareness.

The history of fire in California can be summed up thus: The first inhabitants employed fire, the second avoided it, and we, the third, have tried to stop it.

Fire Management

Wildfire suppression has a legacy in California, and it can never be completely dismantled. But much of the fire policy of yesteryear is changing. The many land managers are switching their focus from prevention to protection. Maybe we are maturing as a state.

The California Department of Forestry and Fire Protection (CDF) has the largest effect on fire policy. In September 2004, the California senate and governor amended a CDF law, increasing the amount of defensible space that must be maintained by homeowners. Community members across the state have started grassroots organizations aimed at increasing public education and reducing fuel. Even the use of prescribed burns to control fuels is on the rise. Many Californians realize that trying to stop a fire will not protect them. But there's another reason for the shift in fire policy—economics.

Wild landscapes that previously were used by industries such as logging and ranching have become attractive to

Some of the benefits of the prescribed burn pictured above include healthy new growth, an increase in the diversity of fauna and flora, and the possibility of lowering the intensity of the next fire.

tourists and homeowners. The value of these landscapes is no longer found in the amount of resources sitting on them, but in the natural beauty of the landscapes themselves. Radiating out from urban centers across the state, property values are higher in areas of natural open space. Marin County and Malibu are excellent examples of places where large tracts of land are maintained to preserve a natural state. Wise fire management preserves tourism dollars, home prices, and nature.

Paying out claims that have exceeded $2 billion a year, insurance companies are also taking a stronger stand. They have increased premiums, sponsored community education programs, and have even threatened to leave certain areas—all of which has led concerned homeowners to take action. Some companies are beginning to use the condition of a property to determine premiums: People with firescaped gardens and fire-resistant building materials and roofs are rewarded with lower rates.

The state has a large incentive to change policy, too. Suppression costs grow proportionally to the amount of people in fire-risk areas, and people are still heading to the hills in large numbers.

In spite of these changes, the shift in fire policy has been slow, and there is still much to do. For fire protection to assume a larger role in California's fire-prone communities, resources and responsibility need to shift. Fire agencies must implement stronger educational programs, employing experts in horticulture and land management, and individuals should assume more responsibility for their safety and the condition of the landscapes that surround them.

There are three ways protect yourself and your property from wildfire: Burn the landscape, manually remove the flammable vegetation, or build a home that will allow a fire to burn around it. Which tactic you and your community employ depends on many factors. The next chapter helps individuals and communities decide which approach is best for their landscape.

But if nothing else, Californians' shift in policy—how we view fire, prescribed burns, and vegetation management—shows signs of maturity. Collectively, we are beginning to understand that fire cannot be stopped in California. Slowly, we are learning to live with it.

The Effects of Wildfire Suppression

Years of successful wildfire suppression have had a large impact on California's landscapes. One plant community blends with another, blurring individual distinctions. Without regular fires, many forests have become old, decadent, and infested. Despite all the fire-suppression efforts, fire remains.

Most of the wildfires today do not have the stimulating effect they once did. Since wildfire-suppression efforts started, many plant communities have missed anywhere from two to 10 natural fire cycles, depending on the area's topography and type of plants. As a result, large tracts of land with dead and dying plants provide ripe fuel for fires that do come through. Plant communities are often dense, in poor health, and invaded by flammable, exotic plants, which create even more volatile situations. When a fire eventually finds fire-suppressed communities, it no longer runs, but rages through the landscape, often killing and sterilizing everything in its path.

Concerns about fire suppression are not new to California. In 1896 John Muir wrote: "Since the fires that formerly swept through the valley have been prevented, the underbrush requires much expensive attention.... . The underbrush and young trees will grow up as they are growing in Yosemite, and unless they are kept under control, the danger from some chance fire, from lightning, if from no other sources, will become greater from year to year. The larger trees will then be in danger."

Before the extensive suppression efforts of today, wildfires would burn and smolder for months at much lower temperatures. Like the 1996 Ackerson Complex fire in Yosemite, where federal officials let the fire run and die naturally, these regular, less intense burns thinned out weaker plants, reducing competition for scarce water and nutrients. Regular and cooler fires also leave more litter behind, which helps slow erosion and build soil fertility. In the past, a wildfire was not necessarily an event to fear.

Today, any small, less severe fire is immediately extinguished. As a result, during the extremes of low humidity and high temperatures, California can expect major conflagrations. Today's wildfires burn with greater intensity, create their own winds, are able to start fires miles away, and increase the chance of severe erosion after they pass. Distressingly, firefighters are rarely able to defeat a conflagration alone; rather, these fires are extinguished when the weather pattern shifts or the fuel runs out.

Chapter 2

Knowing the Terrain

Along Sir Francis Drake Drive, heading toward West Marin and the Point Reyes area, there is a sign near Samuel P. Taylor State Park that reads WOOD AND DEBRIS—LET IT BE. Farther down the road is another sign that indicates the degree of fire danger for the immediate area, which on any typical summer day says HIGH. Both signs along this scenic drive warrant sympathies and actions, yet both have intentions that contradict each other. Which sign do you act upon, and where?

The conflicting ideals that West Marin residents must wrestle with can be found throughout the state. Leaving debris on a forest's floor sets off an ecological chain of events. It may lead to rich soil and an eventual fern-dale, or it may become fuel for a ground fire. Both outcomes can be equally beneficial in the right landscape. However, there are places where this type of unpredictability is harmful, particularly in urban environments.

This chapter looks at these tough issues and presents a simple classification system that can be used to address them. It has been designed so that individuals and communities can begin to define tangible borders, making distinctions between the landscapes where debris is beneficial, and those where it is not. It also will help you determine what type of firescaping is appropriate for your property and surrounding landscape.

Once you define the boundaries of your landscape, you will have a starting point for negotiating a firescaping plan with your family, neighbors, community associations, or government agencies. The plan includes the scope of work: What does fire protected mean in your neighborhood? It includes plant selection: What type of plants support the integrity of the place? And it assigns responsibility: Who is going to do the work, and who is going to pay for it?

After the important decisions have been made, it is time to turn to the remaining chapters. Your immediate risk, design ideas, best plants, and maintenance priorities are some of the topics covered to help you maintain a protected property.

The Three Types of Landscapes

California's landscapes are divided into three broad categories: native, natural, and domestic. These categories are designed to help individuals and communities identify the type of region they live in, in order to develop a plan to minimize their risk of fire damage. These categories describe regions where human actions should be the force that defines the character of the landscape, versus areas where nature should continue to be the dominant force; where people are in charge managing the amount of fuel in a landscape, and where nature manages it.

The Native Landscape

The native landscape is one whose character continues to be developed by environmental forces, such as fires, freezes, floods, erosion, and storms. Humans play an indirect role in influencing the landscape, and it is virtually undeveloped. The plants and animals found in this landscape may be highly specialized, and can include the animals that may pose a risk to humans, such as mountain lions and black bears.

The land manager decides whether a landscape is native. More often than not, these landscapes are publicly protected, and land-management practices are aimed at minimizing human impact. Natural law, as opposed to human will, shapes the nature of the landscape, as well as the public's perception of it. In this landscape, nature rules: Bears come before campers, who must stow their food in animal-proof containers; endangered species can stop logging and development; and roads or trails may be closed to protect an ecosystem that is regenerating. The needs of fauna and flora trump all others.

The native landscape represents some of the most stunning landscapes in California, if not the world. They might include 17 national forests, 30 national parks, 40 wildlife refuges, 40 wilderness areas, more than 50 preserves managed by nongovernment organizations, and 278 state parks.

But the native landscape does not have to be large or remote. It can be near or even surrounded by cities. Tecolote Canyon Natural Park, Santa Rosa Plateau Ecological Reserve, Laguna Coast Wilderness Park, Chino Hills State Park, Cerro San Luis Natural Reserve, Pogonip Open Space Preserve, Wildcat Canyon Regional Park, and Terra Linda/Sleepy Hollow Open Space Reserve are just a few of the many native landscapes nestled next to developed areas.

Fire is inevitable in the native landscape. Historically, fires in these regions were beneficial. They kept plant fuels low and also helped maintain a high level of plant and animal diversity. Whether fire is still beneficial is a current source of debate. Many argue that because of the incredible fuel levels in these regions, wildfires would sterilize the landscape instead of rejuvenating it. Others argue that maintenance of a native landscape requires native processes, and that fire must be returned, sterilized landscapes or not. Either way, nature is a stronger force than humans in the native landscape, and therefore people must adapt to nature's conditions.

When building in the native landscape, that means designing and maintaining structures so that fires can

The unique character of the native landscape shown above has evolved from environmental forces over millennia. Unfortunately, humans have taken fire out of this landscape and it poses a threat to all other landscapes around it. As seen in the picture, the mixed evergreen forest is marching up the hill, increasing the amount of plant fuels while lowering the area's diversity.

burn around them. Typically, these structures are isolated from community resources. Owners must have the capacity to defend their properties against wildfires, without help from others.

To effectively maintain the health of the native landscape, the conditions that influenced its development must be restored. This may require isolating a landscape from urban influences and letting natural events occur, such as fires and floods. Like the native Californians, land managers are using fire with increasing frequency in native landscapes. Encouraging the landscape's naturally occurring cycles will promote indigenous plants and animals, help eliminate aggressive exotic plants, and keep plant fuels from building to conflagration levels.

The Natural Landscape

In the natural landscape, humans have used roads, drains, buildings, and poles to dominate the environment. In spite of this, nature is still in charge of maintaining the landscape. This combination makes the natural landscape the most dangerous of them all.

The natural landscape lacks regular maintenance, and the vegetation cover is comprised of any plant that can survive and reproduce. Located between houses, on vacated properties, and in large, isolated swaths of open space, this landscape can be of any size. It is a hybrid because it exists along with humans and has a combination of native and introduced plants. The plants and animals found in this area are not as specialized as the ones in the native landscape, and they can adapt to a wide range of environments. Animals include possums, skunks, raccoons, and deer.

The natural landscape is typically on city or county land. Mill Valley, Ojai, and Julian are wonderfully charming cities that are dominated by natural landscapes. Each city backs up to large parcels of protected land, and their unique character is drawn from these areas. Natural landscapes are also common in hilly communities where lot sizes are more than half an acre.

Most shoreline communities in California are natural and have gone through multiple manmade changes in the last 200 years. Though they are inland, places such as Clear Lake, Lake Tahoe, and Big Bear share many of the flammable characteristics of their coastal cousins, which include most communities north of Santa Monica.

A natural landscape will commonly blend into a native landscape. In the natural landscape, human concerns outweigh those of the fauna and flora, and yet environmental forces still play a large role in determining its character. This landscape is highly fire suppressed, but poorly maintained, making it highly flammable. Water and wind damage from winter storms are common.

The goal for people in a natural landscape is to maintain high accessibility, usefulness, and safety. Each homeowner is responsible for removing excess fuels on their property, contributing to an overall state of reduced flammability for the community. Community pathways must be clearly marked and maintained. Service and fire roads must be kept clear. Diseased, dying, or dangerous vegetation must be continually removed. Rivers, storm drains, and gutters should be kept clear and clean. The natural landscape has to safely serve the unique goals of the people living in it.

Maintaining a natural landscape can be complex. Sometimes landowners are absent or apathetic. Sometimes a community lacks the funds for massive cleanup projects. And sometimes a community has the money, but public debate keeps anything from happening. But one thing is for sure: The safety of humans in this landscape must outweigh all other goals.

Plant fuels must be kept low. Accomplishing this will require either prescribed burns or regular clearing. Prescribed burns can take place under trees and on small lots, and it is a relatively inexpensive way to clear large areas at a time. However, getting public support is often difficult. Manually clearing and/or thinning is easier to sell the public, but it typically costs more, favors nonnative plants and animals, and can cause erosion on slopes. Either approach used to maintain this landscape will require consistency and community involvement.

This northern California hillside community is surrounded by a natural landscape. Oak, bay, madrone, and Douglas fir are intermixed with acacia, Monterey cypress, eucalyptus, and many other nonnative trees and shrubs. The density, plant type, and age of this landscape make it a dangerous place to live.

The Domestic Landscape

The domestic landscape is planned and regularly maintained. Environmental influences, such as fire, floods, and winds, have the least impact on these well-tended landscapes. The domestic landscape exists because of humans, and in most cases it is dependent upon humans. Examples include front yards, road medians, city parks, and even orchards.

A domestic landscape that lacks regular maintenance will become a natural landscape, and the plants on it will be comprised of anything that can survive and reproduce. The once-flourishing mining towns of the Sierra used to be surrounded by domestic landscapes, rich in a mosaic of livestock, orchards, and crops.

Logging towns of the northern coast were like this, too. But as these towns aged, their lands became less productive and were allowed to overgrow. Now, nature manages the landscapes around many of these historic towns, making them more flammable than typical domestic landscapes.

However, not all domestic landscapes are safe from fire. For a variety of good reasons, many homeowners plant and maintain multiple layers of ornamental vegetation. A dense landscape can help regulate the temperature, buffer unwanted noise, and, perhaps most importantly, provide a greater degree of privacy. Some of these places, such as gothic and alpine-like landscapes, also tend to be flammable because of their use of conifers.

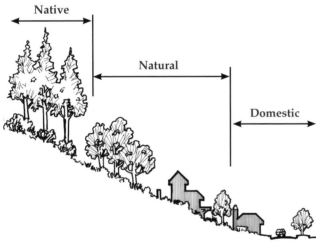

The three landscape categories are deceptively simple. While they are easy to grasp, they are difficult to employ. Distinguishing these landscapes and maintaining them will test the fortitude of any community wishing to stop fire from entering their borders.

Protecting Your Community

The history of fire suggests that it cannot be stopped or suppressed, only delayed. If we cannot lower the likelihood of a fire, we should start concentrating on lowering the intensity of future fires. In the native landscape, and to a lesser degree in the natural landscape, lowering the intensity means raising the frequency; fire must be welcomed back to these landscapes. In California, a native landscape that does not have fire will become a natural landscape, and the conditions for a major conflagration will evolve.

However, structure loss is most common in natural landscapes. Community participation and individual responsibility must replace fire as the dominant force. Strong public education programs are needed. Fire officials and community leaders must overcome negative misconceptions and inform citizens that prescribed burns and manual clearing are good not only for nature, but for them as well.

Perhaps the largest impact people can have in a community is to create and maintain their own fire-protected property. A firescape can be created and maintained to protect a home in any type of landscape—native, natural, or domestic. You, the individual homeowner, need to take action to prevent wildfire from destroying your property, your treasures, your life. The following chapters provide tips and instructions to help you efficiently maintain your landscape. These guidelines promote safety as well as landscape health—like humans and fire, the two can peacefully coexist.

Chapter 3

Determining the Risk of Fire

Ask Marin County residents about the chance of a wildfire in their region, and they'll tell you that Mt. Tamalpais is a powder keg waiting to blow. Ask people living in Trinity, Santa Cruz, or Tahoe counties, and they will say that the risk for them is just as high. If the odds of fire are known, why do we continue to see so much fire damage every year?

Life is full of risks—real and imagined—to our safety and well-being. Our evolutionary reaction is to focus all of our attention on what we perceive to be the most immediate threats. We block thoughts of future possibilities to prevent us from getting distracted. It's a survival strategy, meant to keep us alive during a crisis. But this kind of thinking has dire consequences when used to make everyday decisions—about work, our families, our health, or our houses. We gloss over the long-term impact of poorly made decisions or inaction. We delude ourselves into thinking, "But that won't happen to me." We neglect to consider the real costs of our shortsightedness.

We need to reframe our approach to fire risk. Are the pictures of early childhood worth cutting weeds twice a year? Is a pet's life worth cleaning the roof? And what about decades' worth of other treasures—are any of these things worth taking the time and energy to remove flammable trees? Of course, all of these things are extremely valuable. It's just that our brains do not pose the questions in this manner.

Risk of loss can be calculated in two ways: in terms of how much we have to lose, and in terms of the likelihood of losing it. By assessing your belongings, you can determine the first part of that equation—how much you have to lose. The easy-to-use test in this chapter will help you determine your property's risk of fire—or the likelihood of losing your belongings. It will also evaluate the landscape's ability to attract firefighters. This chapter identifies the environmental and cultural contributions that are the unseen influences to the increase of risk. It

Perspectives: John Garamendi, Insurance Commissioner of the State of California

I grew up on a ranch and I have a ranch. On my folks' ranch and on my ranch, I have fought seven fires. We never lost a structure.

My advice: Prepare to evacuate wherever your home is, in the center of the city or in the boondocks. Know the escape route, know where you are meeting your family, and know what you want to take with you if you have to leave. On the insurance side, take a video camera and go through your home and describe what's there: If you know the cost of it, describe it. If you know where you got it, describe it. Make two copies of the video and send one to [a family member] and keep one with you. It terminates debates with your insurance company. Finally, make sure you have enough insurance to rebuild.

There will always be fires, and now people are [living] where the fires are. Get ahold of a U.S. Geological Survey map of San Diego County from 1900 to date, and you'll see that the area that was burned last time [in 2003] has burned three to four times in the past. This is not unusual; in fact, it is normal. What's changed now is there are homes there. [There are] 35 million Californians and we're spreading out into the woodland-interface areas.

Be prepared for a natural disaster. Earthquakes are common. Fires are common. In some parts of the state, flooding is common. Be prepared, both in terms of personal safety [and] preparing for evacuation, and have adequate insurance.

also provides the characteristics that make a community more or less fire prone and dangerous.

Once you have clearly defined the odds, you can create a plan of action. The remaining chapters are designed to aid in this process. However, knowing your risk doesn't necessarily lead to action—you have to keep asking the right questions and looking ahead to what is really important.

What's Your Risk Level?

The test that follows provides a fairly accurate gauge of the chance of a wildfire consuming a structure. While a variety of factors influence ignition, five play a dominant role: defensible space, outlying areas, degree of slope, exposure, and emergency access.

To determine your risk, answer the questions below and add up your points: The higher the total points, the greater the risk of fire. While providing an overall picture of a property's flammability, this gauge also helps identify the riskiest parts of your property.

Defensible Space

This is undoubtedly a landscape's greatest contributor to a home's chance of survival. Choose the description that best describes the landscape within 30 feet of your structure or home:

- **Domestic gardens, areas that are well tended and watered.**   1 point
- **Wild, uncut grasses.**   3 points
- **Dense and poorly maintained shrubs and trees.**   5 points

Outlying Areas

Outlying areas can greatly influence the chance of your home or structure's survival, especially if the property is sloping and/or the house is old. Based on the outer perimeter, 30 to 100 feet from a structure, score a landscape according to:

- **Landscape that is cleared of dead material. Trees and shrubs are isolated by a distance of two times their height.**   1 point
- **Wild grasses intermixed with poorly maintained shrubs. The shrubs comprise no more than one third of the grassy landscape.**   2 points
- **A dense strand of poorly maintained shrubs or a landscape under a grove of trees (understory) that is regularly maintained.**   3 points

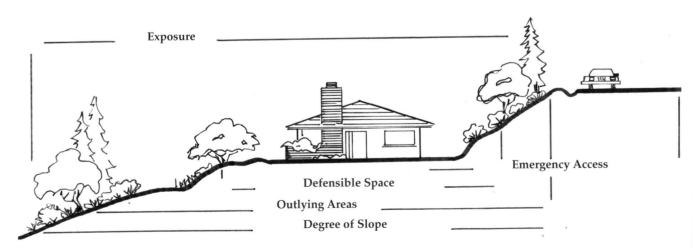

The five factors that most influence a structure's chance of ignition are defensible space, outlying areas, degree of slope, exposure, and emergency access.

- **A landscape that is poorly maintained with many shrubs and trees and a lot of dead vegetation. Also, a dense understory or wooded landscape.**   5 points

Degree of Slope

Degree of slope has an enormous influence on the severity of a fire. Fires run up hills quickly, preheat fuels farther up, produce long flames, and are able to leap over cleared areas. To determine the percentage of a slope, see page 125, and then choose the category below that best describes the degree of slope on your property:

- **A flat surface to a 10% slope.**   1 point
- **Slopes 11–30%.**   3 points
- **Slopes greater than 30%.**   5 points

Exposure

Exposure is the sun's influence on a site. The hotter the site, the more ignitable the property becomes. Choose from:

- **Northeast-facing landscape.**   1 point
- **Northwest-facing landscape.**   2 points
- **Southeast-facing landscape.**   3 points
- **Southwest-facing landscape.**   4 points

Emergency Access

Emergency access is critical in determining a structure's chance of survival during a wildfire. Typically, firefighters will drive only on a street or into a driveway if other cars can drive by and if the fire engine has an area to turn around. Choose from the following descriptions of the street leading to the structure on your property:

- **Two lanes.**   1 point
- **Single lane.**   3 points
- **Single lane that is narrow, curvy, and/or has dense vegetation on either side.**   5 points

Typical in hillside communities, this small road is lined with dense vegetation and overhanging branches. Firefighters would not travel any farther down this road in a fire, leaving the four houses beyond defenseless.

Which description best describes the driveway leading to the structure on your property?

- **It is large enough for a fire engine, and trees and shrubs are removed at least 6 feet past the pavement.**   1 point
- **It is small and narrow, or with dense vegetation on either side.**   3 points
- **It does not access the house.**   5 points

Additional Factors

Additional factors influencing a structure's chance of survival are outlined below. Add the appropriate points if a structure possesses any of the following characteristics:

- **A roof littered with branches and dried leaves.**   1 point
- **A tree overhanging a chimney by 10 or fewer feet.**   2 points

CHAPTER 3

- **The house is more than 1,000 feet from a fire hydrant, or 5 miles or more from a fire station.**   **2 points**
- **The house is 20 years or older.**   **2 points**
- **The house has unprotected areas, such as decks, that overhang a slope.**   **3 points**
- **The house has a wood-shingle roof.**   **5 points**

Score

After totaling the points, use the following chart to calculate a structure's risk of ignition:

- **6–15 points** = **Low risk of fire.**
- **16–23 points** = **Medium risk of fire.**
- **24–35 points** = **Moderately high risk of fire.**
- **36–44 points** = **Dangerous situation with a high risk of fire.**

Environmental Risk Factors

Environmental contributions are the forces that are largely out of our control. They are broken down into three broad categories: climate, pests, and people. While a climatic extreme, such as a prolonged freeze along the coast, can cause massive dieback, not all environmental forces are as persuasive, and most usually work in concert with others. The thread that ties all the forces together is their ability to create either plant fuels or deadwood.

Surrounded by eucalyptus and its litter, this deck will definitely ignite during a wildfire. The deck is unskirted and will catch all the heat, sparks, and wind that the fire creates. A skirt is a barrier, such as plywood and metal sheeting, which runs from the bottom of the deck to the ground.

The dead branches hanging in this Monterey cypress were caused by an unusually strong winter storm. If not cleaned, this tree will be a firetrap, catching wind-blown sparks while providing them with readily ignitable fuel.

The 2003 San Bernardino fire is a quintessential example of how environmental influences created a disaster. Decades of air pollution and many years of drought severely weakened the mature landscape. Almost defenseless, trees and shrubs became hosts to a variety of pests, the most aggressive of which was the western pine-bark beetle. Because fire—the landscape's best defense against pests—had been suppressed, the pests weakened and killed vegetation. That dead and dying vegetation eventually became a rich source of fuel for the fire. The conflagration that ensued destroyed 1,003 homes, and a change in the weather enabled the firefighters to put it out.

Climate

Climatic extremes are the many conditions that create deadwood and set the stage for a major fire. In a natural landscape, these extremes have a far greater impact due to the large amount of poorly adapted and unmaintained plants. A properly maintained domestic landscape will be the least affected by these seasonal extremes.

Some climate factors that influence conditions for fire include:

- **Heavy rains:** Rains increase the growth and proliferation of grasses. These "flash fuels" are quick to ignite and can rapidly spread a fire. Although a wet winter will initially lower the ignitability of trees and shrubs, it encourages more growth than usual and increases the amount of plant fuel for a future fire.

The Odds

According to the *Los Angeles Times,* a review of structures in the path of the 2003 San Diego Cedar fire, which burned down 2,820 homes, revealed the following statistics:

- 90% of the surviving homes had flammable vegetation removed up to 30 feet from around the houses.
- 66% of the surviving homes had flammable vegetation removed up to 10 feet past the houses.
- 60% of the destroyed homes had composition roofs.
- 20% of the destroyed homes had tile or ceramic roofs.
- 45% of the destroyed homes had wood siding.

After the 1981 Atlas fire, the Lake-Napa Ranger Unit of the California Division of Forestry collected the following data:

- 95.5% of the surviving homes had brush cleared around the houses.
- 43.5% of the surviving homes had partial clearance.
- 86.5% of the destroyed or damaged homes had no brush clearance.

This house has all the characteristics of a "loser." Wood shake roof, leaf litter on the roof, tree branches growing under the eaves, fuel ladders and pathways, and the dense vegetation surrounding the house will make it difficult, if not impossible, to save from a wildfire.

• **Seasonal or prolonged drought:** Drought severely weakens plants and causes excess leaf drop and litter. It also prematurely kills older branches, and makes plants more susceptible to pests—all of which increases the ratio of deadwood to live wood.

• **Freezes and prolonged frosts:** Extremely cold weather can cause widespread damage. Killing plants and limbs, these seasonal lows create a lot of deadwood. Injured plants, if they are not pruned, become more susceptible to the effects of drought, heat, wind, and pests, creating even more deadwood years following the initial injury.

• **Uncommonly hot weather:** Heat is a prelude to a big fire. Steaming days suck the moisture from plants and preheat all living and dead plant fuels. The effects of heat become more visible and dangerous as summer fades to autumn. It is this time of year that the moisture content of a plant is at its lowest.

• **Ferocious winter storms:** Storms have an enormous impact on landscapes with a lot of trees. Power failures, road closures, and damage to personal property are inevitable as trees topple and large limbs break. The amount of deadwood that storms create

is astonishing. Older and diseased plants are more prone to storm damage. A storm-damaged landscape is highly susceptible to a variety of pests.

• **Foehn winds:** Dry, hot winds such as Monos and Santa Anas can turn embers into major conflagrations. These foehn winds occur when a high-pressure weather

Fire Weather

Comparing the dates of California's 20 worst fires with the number of Santa Ana wind systems per month provides an interesting look at fire weather. Of the state's 20 worst fires, only two occurred in November, and none was in December. To fan conflagrations, Santa Anas need other factors, such as fuel (plants) with low moisture and hot, dry days. In California, these conditions are common in October, which is why half of the fires occurred in that month. It is by far the most dangerous month of the year.

■ Average Santa Anas per Month   ■ Average Structure Loss per Month

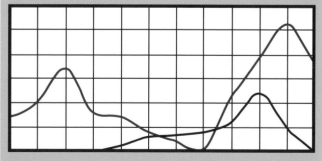

Jan.   Feb.   Mar.   Apr.   May   Jun.   Jul.   Aug.   Sep.   Oct.   Nov.   Dec.

Sources: Protecting Residences from Wildfires: A Guide for Homeowners, Lawmakers, and Planners, *by Howard E. Moore (U.S. Forest Service, May 1981); and the California Department of Forestry.*

CHAPTER 3

Earthquakes and Fire

Six-hundred-and-fifty miles long, 10 miles deep, and possessing hundreds of tributaries, the San Andreas fault has made California more famous than any one movie star. The faultlines shake the state routinely.

There is also a good chance that a quake will start a fire. According to the Federal Emergency Management Agency (FEMA), fire is the most common hazard following an earthquake. The San Francisco quake of 1906 is the quintessential example. It raged for several days and, along with the earthquake, left about half of the city's population homeless. More recently, entire neighborhoods were destroyed by fire after the 1995 earthquake in Kobe, Japan.

The danger posed by earthquake-caused fires is great. During an earthquake, there would be various ignition points and multiple fire fronts. Emergency response would be delayed, if not deterred completely by the broken roads, water supplies, and gas lines. To reduce the risk of fire following an earthquake, take the following steps:

- **Turn off the gas coming into the house.**
- **Turn off the electricity coming into the house.**
- **Open the doors and windows.**
- **Mop up chemical spills.**

Have a professional examine the damage before turning the gas or electricity back on.

A biting freeze a year and a half before this photo was taken caused the dieback seen in this bay tree. An already flammable plant has become even more dangerous because of the freeze. Some researchers suggest that a hard freeze in the winter of 1991 greatly contributed to the ferocity of the Oakland/Berkeley Tunnel fire the following autumn.

system develops in the Great Basin (mountainous, high-desert Nevada and surrounding states), and a weather system of lower pressure moves over the Pacific Ocean. High pressure merges with low and blows the winds toward the ocean. The winds become dry and sometimes hot as they are compressed during their descent from and through the mountains. Humidity can drop as low as 7 percent and wind speeds can climb to 100 mph.

Not all droughts are prolonged, not all summers sweltering, and not all foehns hot. But when any of two these elements combine, and especially when all three do, it's a recipe for disaster. If a fire starts on one of these days, it stops only when it runs out of fuel or when the weather changes.

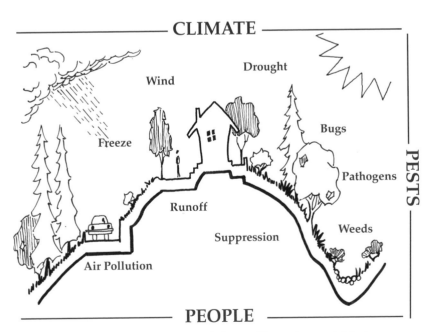

CLIMATE

Wind

Drought

Freeze

Bugs

Pathogens

Runoff

Suppression

Weeds

Air Pollution

PEOPLE

PESTS

The flammability of a property is greatly influenced by environmental factors. With time, the climate, pests, and people can dramatically alter a landscape.

Pests

In a firescaped garden, a pest is anything that adds fuel to the landscape, such as weeds, or anything that increases the amount of deadwood, such as insects, pathogens, or animals.

Weeds include flammable plants, like buckwheat, or aggressive plants, like pampas grass, or both, like broom and mustard. They also displace more desirable, less flammable plants. Another class of weed, the parasite-seed plants, clings onto a host and steals its nutrients, water, and energy. Those include dodder, mistletoe, and witchweed. For a better understanding of weeds, see Chapter 6.

The bark beetle is feverishly hated in California because it is our most destructive insect, in our most cherished landscape, the native landscape. There are several hundred species throughout the United States, and many of them are found in California. Bark beetles attack conifers, such as pines and redwoods, as well as California buckeyes, elms, fruit trees, and oaks. The number of beetles and the ensuing damage are greatly influenced by the health of

Western Pine-Bark Beetle

The western pine-bark beetle (*Dendroctonus brevicomis*) attacks a wide range of pines that are overaged or stressed from other factors, such as a drought or freeze. The beetle targets unhealthy plants and usually spreads to healthy ones only as its population swells.

The first sign of beetle infestation is the presence of dust along the trunk and base. The second indicator is a shotgun pattern of small and sometimes inconspicuous holes at mid-trunk. The only offense against the beetle is a good defense; not much can be done once a pine is infested. If the beetle is spotted early, your best bet is to remove the damaged area and nurture the tree. If the entire tree is infested, you should remove it during the coldest part of the year, which should stop the beetle from migrating to other pines during the process.

its host. A healthy tree can defend against and live with beetles; a weakened tree cannot. Age, drought, rot, and air pollution can debilitate trees, creating conditions that support large beetle populations.

A pathogen is any microorganism that can cause disease. And diseases, like oak root fungus, can make a fire-resistant plant fire prone. Dieback, leaf drop, and poor recovery from injury are some of the symptoms of fungus and the reasons they increase flammability. The effects of these pathogens are as diverse as the pathogens themselves. In most cases, the type of host, its health, and the environment around it determines the type of pathogen and the amount of damage it causes. For example, coastal fog that persists longer than normal creates the ideal incubator for mildews, molds, rusts, and root rot. Bark beetles and other boring insects provide an entry point for fungi, and these pathogens are as much to blame for the death of the host as are the beetles.

The effect of animals on fire risk varies with their habits, population size, and habitat. In a wooded landscape, for example, when the number of deer rises, the flammability of that area increases as well. That's because the deer begin competing for food and eat everything in the area except for the vegetation they find distasteful—particularly plants with small, hard, hairy, and resinous leaves. These also happen to be the most flammable plants. Therefore, a landscape becomes increasingly fire prone as a deer population grows in wooded areas.

The deadwood and oozing sap seen on the pine tree above is caused by pine-bark beetles. This tree is nearly dead. The longer this pine remains standing, the more likely the pest will spread to other pines. This tree should be removed when the beetles are least active, during winter or early spring.

Sudden Oak Death Syndrome

This well-known disease may not be aptly named because it attacks a wide range of plants and death is rarely sudden. The fungus responsible for sudden oak death syndrome *(Phytophthora ramorum)* was identified in Marin County in 1995, and presently there may be tens of thousands of trees infected, from Big Sur to Mendocino County and all the coastal ranges in between.

Of the oaks, the coast live, black, and Shreve are the most affected. The fungus is also known to attack big leaf maple, California bay, California buckeye, California huckleberry, madrone, manzanita, rhododendron, tan bark oak, and toyon. Some evidence suggests that that the redwood may be susceptible, too.

In oaks, the symptoms of this disease include seeping along the trunk and whole branches losing their leaves at once (hence "sudden"). However, those ailments are similar to those caused by other pests, and positive identification requires a pathological examination. Indicators of the disease on the other plants include leaf spots, dying patches, or lesions and branches losing all of their leaves.

Unfortunately, there is no cure. As with all fungi, the disease typically thrives in warm and moist environments, even in domestic gardens. Shady areas with poor air circulation are ideal incubators for fungi. If you spot a fungus-infected plant, prune or remove it, or isolate it to a sunny spot so it can dry out. Also, it is important to let a native garden completely dry during summer, its natural period of rest.

In a grassy, weedy landscape, large populations of grazing animals have a different effect on the landscape. There are grazers, such as goats, that find almost everything on a landscape palatable—including poison oak. These animals can dramatically reduce the amount of grasses, small perennials, and supple shrubby plants. But there are also many concerns about using them, most of which center around erosion. Grazing dislodges soil particles and reduces the vegetation cover that would normally buffer the effects of wind and rain. Topsoil loss is not uncommon.

However, there are ways of managing grazing animals that will lower the fire risk in summer and minimize the liability of erosion in winter. When their population is kept balanced through careful ranch management, they will help lower the risk of fire. Grazing can encourage new plant growth, which is moist and supple, without eradicating or promoting one specific type of plant. Using grazing animals for vegetation management is examined in Chapter 6.

People

People have an enormous effect on the landscapes around them; indeed, a full discussion of humans' environmental impact on nature is beyond the scope of this book. The human-created factors listed below—air pollution, runoff, levels of ground water, and fire suppression—increase the flammability of a site.

Air pollution—ozone, sulfur oxides, and the other noxious gases released by combustion engines—affects plants in several ways. It lowers productivity and photosynthesis, and it weakens resistance to droughts, insects, and diseases. Air pollution and the attendant plant stress are prevalent in the large valleys of California, which also happen to be prime growing regions. Not all plants react the same; birch, pine, and sycamore are more easily injured by dirty air.

One reason why the natural landscape is California's most dangerous is runoff. When water and nutrients bleed into the natural landscape from the surrounding domestic landscapes, the natural landscape becomes much more productive, which leads to a large leap in fuels. Many of the plants that these landscapes support are poorly adapted to California's climatic extremes, and are more prone to damage as a consequence.

A lot of water travels underground in California, and many water-starved communities rely on this resource to meet their needs. Pulling water from the ground and channeling water away from a watershed lowers the water table. This lower table is visible along the foothills and watershed corridors. While droughts get the bulk of the blame for our dry landscape, retreating groundwater supplies contribute greatly.

Ironically, fire suppression is a major cause of conflagrations. Prior to the influx of white settlers in the mid-1800s, fires were much more common. These regular fires kept fuels low and the landscape in a constant state of rebirth and growth. The fires today do not have the stimulating effect they once had. The history and effects of suppression are covered in more detail in Chapter 1.

CHAPTER 3

Dug back into the hill, this driveway is sure to attract firefighters. It can accommodate a fire engine and all the equipment necessary to defend the home. The vegetation surrounding the driveway is properly maintained as well.

Characteristics of a Hazardous Community

There are many characteristics that make a particular neighborhood or community more dangerous during a wildfire. These factors hinder emergency response and swift evacuation, contribute to the buildup of fuels, and help push a fire through a community.

Canyons and Valleys

Winds become compressed and stronger when pushed through narrow areas, making canyons and valleys particularly fire prone. Many of California's most devastating fires, such as the Oakland/Berkeley Tunnel fire in 1991 and Laguna's fire in 1993, originated in canyons. Firefighters typically battle a blaze at the tops of canyons and valleys, making the homes mid-slope defenseless and vulnerable.

Open Spaces Between Houses

Parcels of open space are common in suburban and rural areas. These natural landscapes can be between 100 square feet and 20 square acres, and more often than not they are fire suppressed, poorly maintained, and pose a significant risk to the structures that are nestled within them.

Emergency Access

In hillside communities with narrow streets, evacuation and emergency response can be seriously impaired. Fleeing residents compete against arriving emergency vehicles, clogging the streets and slowing everyone's progress. Narrow, winding streets are common in old, unplanned foothill communities.

Water Supply and Distribution

Undersized and old water mains can limit the water supply for firefighting. Individuals living above a water reservoir may be in serious danger if the pump that supplies their water is powered by the same electrical source that their homes use. Some older hillside communities have outdated water systems that have not had seismic improvements, creating a highly dangerous situation if a fire is started by an earthquake.

Attracting Firefighters

During a wildfire, emergency personnel have to decide whether they will defend a particular home. Firefighters are under orders not to risk their lives for homes and properties that pose a significant risk to themselves, which are typically those in obvious states of neglect. Firefighters call these properties "losers." The secret to attracting firefighters during a wildfire is creating a safe haven that beckons them. The following characteristics increase the appeal of your home and property to firefighters:

- A large driveway that allows fire trucks to easily drive to a house.
- A house that has removed flammable vegetation 100 feet from all sides.
- A nonflammable and easily accessible roof.
- A house with no open gables (a roof that extends over a house).
- Screened vents and skirted decks overhanging a slope.
- An area where equipment can be laid out.
- Easy-to-use paths around a house.
- Gas tanks with defensible space around them.
- Thinned vegetation surrounding defensible space.
- Resources that will help firefighters battle a fire, such as stored water, water pumps, shovels, hoes, and ladders.

CHAPTER 3

Communication

In fire-prone hillside communities, communication is necessary but difficult. A majority of these areas do not have emergency sirens, or if they do, the sirens may be hard, if impossible to hear. Since communication is the key to a successful response, sirens should be installed at frequent intervals and wired to an independent power supply. Many rural communities have put in their own emergency radio stations, which appears to be one of the best ways to rapidly transmit local information.

Personal Preferences

Despite the real and known risk of fire, many individuals are hesitant to remove dense vegetation and flammable plants. The human influences that add fuels to a landscape are the cultural contributions to the risk of fire. These contributions are the unseen barriers to fire protection. For a firescaped garden to be successful, these human elements must be addressed. Below are some of reasons why dense vegetation persists in fire-prone communities.

The pursuit of privacy is one of the biggest detractors to fire safety, especially in this era of high-density housing developments. For this reason, people are hesitant to remove barrier vegetation, and instead add to the fuel load by planting and sheering vines, trees, and large shrubs and building fences. Privacy must be planned for in a firescaped garden.

Plants provide comfort. Trees and shrubs help regulate temperatures, buffer wind and noise, and can drench the air with intoxicating scents. There a lot of reasons why people keep vegetation close to them: Plants make people feel good.

Perspectives: David Carmany, California
Homeowners Insurance Product Manager, AAA

For homeowners in California, firescaping is one of the best ways to reduce the risk of fire damage to your home and property. But it is not a guarantee against fire damage—especially if you live in a high-risk area. To protect against financial loss that would result from a fire, you also need to get appropriate homeowners insurance.

The greatest catastrophic risks to California homeowners are brushfires and earthquakes that cause fires. Most insurance companies either don't insure homes in brushfire areas, or they insure only homes with adequate defensible space—typically anywhere from 50 to 2,000 feet.

Insurers are becoming more sophisticated in their underwriting and pricing practices. Already, some charge lower rates for nonflammable roofs. This means that homeowners who invest in a nonflammable roof or the creation of defensible space will not only protect their family and belongings, they may also be able to get lower insurance rates.

Below are some tips for insuring your property:

Get an Adequate Limit
The cost to completely rebuild your home in the event of a covered loss is called the coverage A value. Your insurance agent or a contractor can help make sure your coverage A amount is enough to rebuild your home if it is completely destroyed.

Be aware that inflation costs or reconstruction problems may increase the price of rebuilding beyond your policy limit. Approximately 75 percent of total losses exceed 125 percent of the coverage A value stated on the policy. Given this, you may want to consider purchasing limited replacement cost coverage. This increases the limit of insurance, typically to 125 percent of the stated coverage A value, although some insurers offer higher limits such as 150 percent.

Compare Price
When comparing insurance quotes from different carriers, first make sure the coverage A amount is the same.

Buy From a Trustworthy Company
Select a company that keeps its promises and pays claims quickly and without hassle.

Photograph or Videotape Your Home and Belongings
Save the photos online or somewhere away from your home. After a fire, they will help you file an insurance claim.

Hillside properties are not only more fire prone than flat landscapes, they are also more expensive to maintain. Work on slopes is physically demanding, expensive, and sometimes requires the use of experts, which further increases the costs. The difficulties and higher costs of working on slopes helps explain why many hillside properties are neglected and eventually become natural landscapes.

Naturally, an owner's finances have a large effect on the property's risk of fire. Budget constraints can delay regular clearing, pruning, and watering. In some cases, the costs to reduce the hazards are beyond an individual's or a community's resources, abilities, or inclinations. A 60-foot-tall pine tree, for example, can cost $900 to $1,500 to cut down and haul away. Properly placed vegetation can also lower heating and cooling costs, creating an economic incentive to keep them close to a structure.

Earthquakes, fires, and floods—California is geologically dynamic. While most Californians acknowledge the risks, not all act upon them. The fear of change, the misperception of risk, and simple apathy are the biggest barriers to fire protection. Tragically, many people are not motivated to assist in their own survival, despite the likelihood that a major disaster would stretch a community's emergency resources beyond capacity. Although public interest is high after a major disaster, it infrequently leads to sustained action.

Chapter 4

A Model for Home Protection

After almost every wildfire, at least one home survives, somehow protected from the flames that consumed all others. This chapter provides a model that can help your house survive a fire. This model is a set of design and maintenance guidelines developed decades ago and continually improved upon by dedicated scientists and firescaping professionals. Implementing these guidelines is the emphasis of the remaining chapters.

In 1923, Berkeley lost 584 homes in the state's seventh-worst fire. Over the following 50 years, residents of that city not only battled a multitude of smaller fires, they researched and employed the latest in fire science. The amount of analysis written during that time would have filled a classroom, yet none of it helped in 1991, when Berkeley was again hit, this time by the Tunnel fire, the state's most savage fire. The community lacked the action to make the knowledge work.

More than anything, this model needs you. No matter how much we learn about fire, knowledge alone will never save a structure. Only action will.

Firescaping's Zone Theory

Immediately following a slew of fires that destroyed hundreds of post–World War II homes in the Los Angeles foothills in the late 1950s and early 1960s, the Los Angeles Arboretum led a group of conservation agencies, government officials, and local universities in producing

> According to a study reported by the *Los Angeles Times*, of the 2,820 homes that burned down in the 2003 Cedar fire, 66 percent had vegetation growing up to 10 feet around them, which means that possibly 1,518 of the homes destroyed were in violation of state law.

and distributing information about fire protection. It was during this time that the fire zone model was fully developed and adapted as the preferred method for homesite protection. This model, which we still use today, consists of four concentric zones radiating out from a structure. Each zone has a different role in helping to defend a home from a wildfire.

The fire zone model serves as the foundation for firescaping's zone theory, which also has four concentric zones radiating out from a structure. But unlike the model, firescaping addresses the many other demands placed on California landscapes. Planting for a sense of privacy or to stabilize a hillside can inadvertently create a lot of fuel. A good landscape design will not only help defend a home against the threat of fires, it will serve the unique goals of the individuals who care for it.

Every property can benefit from using firescaping's zone theory, but the degree of necessity varies. Houses perched on slopes or those in the middle of native landscapes, especially landscapes that burn on a regular basis, can benefit the most from the zone theory. The greatest precautions should be taken in fire-prone landscapes. However, the theory is not ideally suited for every property. Houses on small lots, built under trees, or located on ridgetops need a tailored approach. Chapter 5 addresses specific situations with design ideas to solve their unique problems.

Reducing the chance of structure loss requires healthy plants, a clean landscape, and ample distance between clusters of plants. These three goals are central to firescaping's zone theory. They are also central to the entire book. A firescaped garden is never created once, but maintained over a lifetime.

The Law and Firescaping

Enacted in 1963, the Public Resources Code for Minimum Statewide Clearance of Brush (also called PRC 4291) sets the minimum standards for homesite protection. Nearly a year after 2003's devastating fire season, Governor Arnold Schwarzenegger signed a bill, SB 1369, that updated and strengthened the existing fire code. Most importantly, this amendment extended the mandated firebreak from 30 feet to 100 feet.

Paraphrased, the new law states that a firebreak must be maintained no fewer than 100 feet around a structure in fire-hazard areas. This firebreak can be extended by the state forester if warranted by hazardous conditions. High fire-hazard areas are defined as any mountainous area or landscape covered in forest, brush, grasses, or other flammable vegetation. A local agency can also designate an area as high fire hazard. If a resident has questions about the area they live in, they can call their local fire district.

A firebreak is made by removing all brush, flammable vegetation, and combustible growth. However, the law does allow that "grasses and other vegetation located more than 30 feet from a structure and less than 18 inches in height can be maintained where necessary to stabilize the soil and prevent erosion." The law also states that vegetation within 10 feet of a chimney outlet must be removed; that trees next to a structure must be kept clear of deadwood; that the roof must be kept clear of debris; that all chimney outlets must have screens; and that new structures must show compliance with all building codes.

While firebreaks are not covered in this book, the recommendations included here exceed state standards. As defined by the current law, the firebreak would fall into zones 1, 2, and 3 of this book's firescaping zone theory. At a minimum, these three zones make recommendations for the landscape that extends 120 feet from a structure. On slopes, the recommendations can reach to 200 feet. When zone 4 recommendations are added, this model extends to the outermost limits of an individual's property. The biggest difference between this book and state law is that *Firescaping* breaks down the concept of a firebreak into many manageable parts, creating action plans for all kinds of challenging environments.

Zone 1: Garden Zone

Distance: Extends 30 feet from all sides of a house or structure.

Primary Goal: The garden zone plays one of the most important roles in fire protection. This zone should be able to withstand flying embers and intense heat of between 900°F to 1,300°F, without igniting. All individuals should be able to move swiftly and safely through the garden zone. Firefighters will battle a blaze within these 30 feet.

Secondary Goals: The garden zone has to retain a high recreational and functional value to remain useful to its occupants. The pursuits of beauty and privacy play large roles in determining plant selection. Fences, hedges, sheds, compost areas, and stored items, such as firewood, are common features that add a lot of fuel to this zone.

Recommendations: The garden zone consumes the most time, water, and nutrients—also known as imports. This is the only zone that should be dependent upon frequent imports. Vegetables, lawns, perennials, and tropical plants are examples of fire-retardant, high-maintenance gardens. However, any type of garden, such as those with native plants, can be kept relatively fire retardant with a continual supply of water, nutrients, and maintenance time.

The best plants for the garden zone are supple, moist, and broadleaf. Trees should be picked with care and need to serve many functions in this small area. These trees should be fire retardant and able to withstand environmental influences, such as wind, heat, and cold; they must not endanger a structure with their roots or limbs.

Since firefighters will battle a blaze within this first perimeter, access to and away from the structure should be continually maintained. In an emergency, a house's occupants will be leaving with their arms full of personal belongings, while firefighters will be rushing personnel and equipment to the structure. Everyone should be able to move easily through the property, without ducking, tripping, or worrying about what's ahead. On larger lots, creating and maintaining two ways off the property is essential.

Keeping the garden zone clean of all ignitable litter is the single most important maintenance task. Because

In 1985, the City of Santa Barbara Fire Department created a firescaped demonstration garden, in response to the 1977 Sycamore Canyon fire, when 234 structures were destroyed. The garden embodies the zone theory and educates residents about how landscaping can improve their chances of surviving a wildfire. Visitors can access the garden at Mission Ridge Road and Stanwood Drive, across from 2411 Stanwood Drive.

What I tell people is to think about a fire coming toward your house and try to look for three things—fire ladders, spacing of vegetation, and total volume of vegetation—that provide a path fire can follow and can increase a fire's intensity. I think with fire-safe landscaping, people focus on the plants. But with me, it's not just the plants; plants are a big part of it, but it is fire ladders and spacing. If you look at the horizontal or vertical continuity of an area, those are the things you are bringing in with your selection of plants. I'm not a plant expert, but I do know fire behavior and that's what I focus on: How is fire going to burn in an area?

We try to really emphasize maintenance, but not everybody gets the point. There are homeowners who are, obviously, very good at brush clearance. If I looked at how many people complied with our brush-clearance standards, I don't think it's more than 10 percent of the people in our high fire-hazard areas. That's not very good. From year to year, maintenance costs would be much less if they kept it up annually.

Lives . . . for me that's the most important thing. The reason for fire landscaping is to protect the public and houses, but most importantly, [it is to save] lives. I think we're seeing more loss of life. We've seen a lot of firefighter loss of life, but we're also starting to see more civilian losses.

The first three houses in this picture were built after the original homes burned down in the 1993 Laguna Beach fire. All three homeowners chose to use different yet effective architectural and landscape design elements to protect themselves. It's likely that all three houses will survive the next fire.

Zone 2: Greenbelt/Fuel Break

Distance: Extends 31 to 70 feet from a protected structure. Houses on slopes need to add an additional 10 feet to this zone for every 10 percent increase in slope. For example, the greenbelt would extend to 120 feet on a property with a 50 percent slope.

Primary Goal: The greenbelt should stop a ground fire. The amount of fuel in this zone greatly affects a structure's chance of surviving a wildfire. Because a fire's flame length and speed doubles with every 10 percent increase in slope, the perimeter must be extended on hills. The effects of climatic extremes, such as droughts and freezes, and occupant neglect should have the least impact in this zone.

Secondary Goals: Within view of a house, privacy, aesthetics, and wind protection play important roles in plant selection and placement. Employing these goals adds a lot of fuel to this zone over time. On sloping properties, controlling erosion is one of the most important roles of this zone.

Recommendations: A majority of the plants in the greenbelt should grow no higher than 18 inches. The plants in this zone must retain their fire retardation despite droughts, freezes, infestations, and possible occupant neglect. Hedges, screens, gas tanks, water tanks, and outbuildings are common features in this zone and should be

of the many features found here, there is typically more fuel found in the garden zone than elsewhere. Places that are likely to produce sparks and heat, such as barbecue areas and driveways, should have all flammable vegetation removed from around them. Continuous lines of plant fuels, such as hedges and vine-covered fences, should be broken up, staggered, and well maintained. See Chapter 5 to create functional, low-fuel fences.

The occupants of this home have taken the time to establish a hillside garden with succulents. This planting scheme is fire retardant, drought tolerant, and low maintenance. It is also choking out the flammable, unwanted vegetation that has invaded the properties nearby.

isolated from fuel pathways. Features such as driveways, community pathways, and roads must be kept clear as firebreaks and emergency exits for residents and firefighters.

The greenbelt is a much larger area to maintain than zone 1, especially on slopes. Due to the relatively large size of the greenbelt, plant fuels have a tendency to accumulate. Weeds are typically a persistent problem and can also add a lot of fuel to this zone. Overcoming constant buildup of plant fuels requires planning.

The goal in designing a greenbelt is to create a low-fuel area that can successfully be grown within the water and maintenance budgets of a particular site. The plants selected should be aggressive enough the choke out flammable and unwanted weeds, but not aggressive enough to move into the natural and native landscapes nearby. Establishing the greenbelt may take two to four years. The work involved in establishing this type of planting may include exhausting the soil of its stored weed seeds, extensive planting/seeding, creating barriers to migrating seeds, installing a watering system, and maintaining a budget for annual cleanup.

Plants for the fuel break should be low growth, low fuel, and low maintenance. Although all plants recommended for this zone are low in fuels, they will only be low maintenance if used in the appropriate location. Low-maintenance plants are compatible with specific site and size requirements. Any plant that requires regular imports, such as water or pruning time, is not low maintenance. Erosion-controlling plants not only have aggressive root systems, but their foliage and branches trail along the soil, helping to hold and protect the soil.

Removing dead, damaged, and diseased vegetation is the most important use of maintenance time. To ensure a successful evacuation and swift emergency response, all paths and driveways should be regularly cleared. Maintaining access throughout this zone not only helps in an emergency, it makes the area more accessible and easier to enjoy. Windbreaks and privacy hedges should be isolated from other large plants and kept in state of good health.

Although the greenbelt will consume the second highest amounts of water, nutrients, and maintenance time, it may not require these imports. Importing nutrients, and to a degree, water, stimulates plants to grow beyond the limitations of the immediate environment. The new, stimulated growth is dependent on the imports and will become stressed and more flammable if the imports are lessened or removed. The goal of water, nutrients, and maintenance time in the greenbelt is not necessarily to create a lot of growth, but to sustain the health of the plantings.

Zone 3: Transition Zone

Distance: Starting at 71 feet from a structure, and much farther on slopes, this zone extends 50 feet outward, to 120 feet on flat ground. On smaller lots, the transition zone may only be a row of barrier shrubs.

Primary Goal: The transition zone should dramatically slow a fire.

Secondary Goals: The transition zone acts as a buffer between zones 2 and 4. This zone should help stop unwanted plants from entering into the greenbelt. Controlling weeds, channeling water, and catching sediment from a property are also important functions. Creating habitat may be important, too. Plant selection becomes less influenced by aesthetics and more by these other goals.

Recommendations: Typically, the work in this zone involves managing the existing vegetation rather than trying to establish a new type of landscape. To help this zone slow a fire, trees and large shrubs should be kept isolated by a width of two times their mature height, wild grasses should be mowed to 6 inches, and vines and shrubs should be removed from under trees.

The transition zone protects the greenbelt from unwanted, flammable weed seeds. Conversely, it protects the native landscape from aggressive exotics. A row of durable barrier shrubs, such as sageleaf rockrose, will help stop the migration of weed seeds and will significantly lower the plant fuels and maintenance requirements of zone 2. Small properties that are adjacent to open space may not have the room for zone 3. However, even a small row of seed-grabbing shrubs, like ceanothus or prostrate coyote brush, or a wire mesh fence, will help separate the native landscape from the domestic gardens, improving the health of both landscapes.

Planting in zone 3 usually has specific purposes: controlling erosion, creating barriers, and enhancing wildlife. Plants selected for the transition area should be low growing, broadleaf, able to survive in native soils, and able to be taken off supplemental water once established. Plants selected for this zone should be more fire resistant than fire retardant. (Fire resistant means a plant can survive and possibly even slow the progress of a fire, but not necessarily stop it.) Many plants recommended for this zone are native and sprout or germinate soon after a fire, minimizing the chances of erosion and aiding in a landscape's recovery.

As in all zones, removing dead, diseased, and damaged vegetation is the single greatest use of maintenance time. Creating and maintaining access throughout this zone is the second highest use of time. For the most part, however, the work in this zone will involve managing the growth, which includes the removal of trees, shrubs, and weeds.

Practical for almost any garden, a lawn is framed by a meadow that requires little time and water to maintain, yet provides a perfect transition to the dense landscape farther out.

Zone 4: Native or Natural Zone/Open Space

Distance: On flat ground, 121 feet from a protected structure and outward. On slopes, this zone starts much farther out.

Primary Goal: The open space should reduce the severity of a fire.

Secondary Goals: Other important goals of this zone are to ensure that the native or natural landscape does not pose unnecessary risk to the individuals living around it, and to maintain the health of a landscape's fauna and flora.

These clever homeowners have inverted the zones and created not only a well-protected garden but community pathways as well. The zone 1 lawn is bordered by zone 2 hill-holding plants, such as ceanothus, ground morning glory, lantana, and artemisia.

Recommendations: Reducing the severity of a fire and the risk fire poses to the people living around zone 4 requires one of two approaches, or their combination, to regulate the accumulation of plant fuels: removal of vegetation (by hand or by machine), and/or prescribed fires.

Although a lot of communities are hesitant to employ fire to control the buildup of plant fuels, it has proven to be an effective approach. Prescribed burns are less expensive than mechanical removal; they promote California's native, fire-adapted plants; and they do not disturb the landscape to the degree that mechanical clearing does, which encourages aggressive, nonnative plants.

There are, however, many landscapes that are either too small or too close to structures to use fire as a method of land management. In the situations where prescribed burns cannot be used, mechanical removal of vegetation is the only option.

In most zone 4 situations, community participation is needed to reduce the severity of a fire. One individual or family can do little to control the massive fuel buildup in California's productive plant communities. Using fire to manage a landscape is controversial and mechanical clearing is costly, and both approaches require community consensus to be effective. Prescribed burns should be used about every 15 years. Mechanical removal will be needed every four to six years.

Plants are not recommended for this zone because planting is rarely necessary. Planting is required only when concerns of erosion outweigh the needs of the native plant community, in which case zone 3 plants are recommended. A list of seeds used to control erosion is provided in Chapter 10.

Characteristics of a Fire-Protected Property

In addition to defensible space and the other important landscaping features described in firescaping's zone theory, there are many other elements that create a fire-protected property. From the type of roofing material to the size of a driveway to the amount of stored water, sometimes it is the small things that add up and influence the chance of survival. As a house and landscape accumulate the characteristics of a protected property, the likelihood of survival increases. Listed below are almost all the characteristics of a fire-protected property: the house, paths, and landscape. Some are easy to acquire, while others take time and money.

The House

A fire-resistant roof, preferably Class A, like metal, clay, or concrete tile, may be the single most important aspect of fire protection.

A house's roof is only slightly slanted, not highly pitched, and follows the direction of the slope.

Easy access to the roof is created and maintained.

Flammable debris, like leaves and twigs, are regularly swept off the roof.

Dried and dead vegetation is removed from under the house and decks.

Firewood is kept 30 feet away and uphill from the house.

Under firescaping's zone theory, each zone's size, purpose, and plant palette will dramatically increase the chance of survival. Second only to roof type, and some data suggest second to none, the landscape surrounding a house has an enormous influence in determining a property's fate during a wildfire.

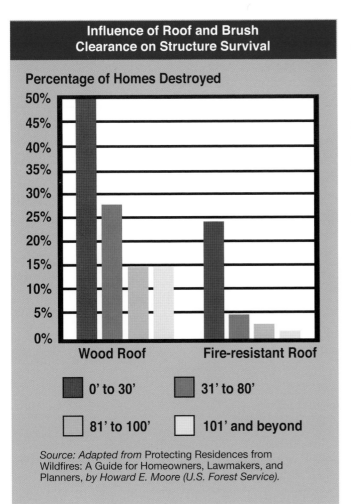

Influence of Roof and Brush Clearance on Structure Survival

Percentage of Homes Destroyed

Legend:
- ■ 0' to 30'
- ■ 31' to 80'
- □ 81' to 100'
- □ 101' and beyond

Source: Adapted from Protecting Residences from Wildfires: A Guide for Homeowners, Lawmakers, and Planners, *by Howard E. Moore (U.S. Forest Service).*

A house's address is clearly visible from both directions along the street.

The underpinning of decks and overhangs are enclosed with a nonflammable skirt, such as concrete blocks, gypsum boards, or metal siding. If a skirt is not used, oversized lumber (for example, 6-by-6-inch beams and posts) should be used for the supporting members, and items that are even slightly ignitable are stored elsewhere.

Eaves are either eliminated or coated with nonflammable material, like stucco.

All air vents are small and screened with mesh that is noncombustible, noncorrosive, and smaller than a quarter inch.

The siding on the house is noncombustible, such as stucco and stone. Any fissures or breaks in the siding are repaired. Wood shingles are avoided. Other types of wood siding have a one-hour fire-resistance rating and are put together so that there are no cracks or fissures.

Every chimney has a spark arrester made from noncombustible and noncorrosive wire mesh with gaps no larger than a half inch.

Decks are made from bricks, tile, or concrete. If wood is used, oversized lumber with a one-hour fire-resistance rating is used. Decks are pieced together using tongue-and-groove design, leaving no gaps between the boards.

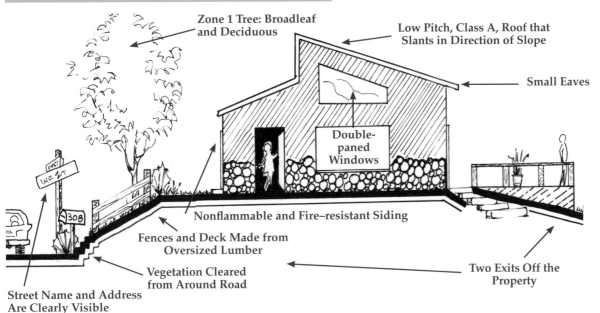

Zone 1 Tree: Broadleaf and Deciduous

Low Pitch, Class A, Roof that Slants in Direction of Slope

Small Eaves

Double-paned Windows

Nonflammable and Fire–resistant Siding

Fences and Deck Made from Oversized Lumber

Vegetation Cleared from Around Road

Street Name and Address Are Clearly Visible

Two Exits Off the Property

Highlighted above are just some of the many characteristics needed to protect a home and family from a wildfire.

CHAPTER 4

Glass windows facing a fire-risk area are small and double- or thermal-paned. At the very least, windows are made with tempered glass. Curtains are replaced with louvers, shutters, or fire curtains.

Access to the House

All roads are maintained as firebreaks, or areas that will help stop the spread of fire.

Vegetation is cleared 10 feet from either side of the road. The plants along the road are either regularly mowed or planted with fire-retardant or fire-resistant ground cover.

The street name and address are clearly visible from both directions along the main road.

Branches are pruned 15 feet above the driveway and roads. Trees and shrubs are removed 10 feet from either side of driveway.

An area that allows large trucks to turn around is created on streets that dead end.

On all properties, including small lots, there are two ways to get off on foot.

The Landscape

No less than 100 feet of easily accessible, defensible space is created and maintained around all structures, as described for zones 1, 2, and 3.

Dead, dying, and diseased vegetation is continually removed.

The plants immediately around a house are maintained to be fire retardant and/or resistant.

Trees and shrubs are maintained so there are no fire pathways (horizontal and continuous lines of plants) or fire ladders (vertical and continuous lines of plants).

Shrubs and trees are isolated by a width of two times their mature height.

Trees limbs are kept 15 feet from a structure and 10 feet above its roof.

All flammable debris and plants are removed 10 feet past the drip line of trees and shrubs.

Walls and fences are made from masonry, wrought iron, chain link, or other nonflammable material. If wood is used, it is oversized lumber with a one-hour fire-resistant rating. Garden features, such as trellises, arbors, and planters, are made with noncombustible materials or oversized lumber.

If large enough, a fuel break should be maintained around a property. Fuel breaks are described in more detail under zone 2.

The emergency water pumps in pools and spas are powered by a diesel, gas, or propane generator. The water pump is no smaller than 100 gpm (gallons per minute) with a standard 1.5-inch outlet. A 100-foot-long, cotton-jacket fire hose is neatly coiled by the water pump. Drainage pipes of pools, spas, and water tanks are readily accessible.

Fire trucks can park to within 10 feet of large water storage areas, such as ponds and cisterns.

Chapter 5

Designing for Fire and Safety

A firescaped garden is not a moonscape, a barren desert, or a severely mowed pasture. A firescaped landscape is anything—anything, that is, but dangerous. A streamside woodlands, flush with ferns and sorrel; a Mediterranean retreat with bougainvillea, palms, and sages; or a garden under a grove of pines, with huckleberry and hazel can be designed and kept fire safe. A firescaped design does not have a particular look, but it can slow the spread of fire and help protect a home and its occupants.

If there is anything that ties all firescaped gardens together, it is the language. Firescaping yells at emergency personnel, but whispers to neighbors; it is easy to read, yet may be reluctant to reveal its secrets; it is constantly working for the property's occupants, but never shows the signs of strain. Firescaped gardens speak volumes about how homeowners view their role within the community.

Included in this chapter are all the elements needed to speak firescaping's vocabulary. You'll find many general design ideas, as well as recommendations for difficult landscapes, such as hillsides, ridgetops, small lots, and understory properties. Lastly, you'll receive guidelines for creating less flammable garden features, such as outbuildings, arbors, fences, and hedges.

General Design Principles

Fire is a natural consequence, and removing it requires energy equal to or greater than it. Gardeners and homeowners possess this energy. A landscape without fire in California is considered natural, not native; human needs outweigh those of fauna and flora. All the recommendations that follow are based on this fundamental principle: We must be the force that defines our landscape.

Keep It Simple

Long after it has been designed and constructed, a firescaped garden has to remain effective. Kids and their many uses for a landscape move out (use lowers flammability), interest wanes, and other pressing crises divert attention. A simple design can accommodate these lapses in attention.

Entrances and Exits

Swift and safe exits are essential. From the parking area, the path leading to a structure should be easily identifiable and navigated, which might mean lighting at night. The slope should not exceed 3 percent downward, but should have a least a 2 percent cross slope, to shed moisture. It should be at least 6 feet wide, and the surface should accommodate wheels. Concrete, wood, crushed rock, or compacted earth work well.

Protect Yourself from Yourself

Sad but true: Our houses are more likely to be burned down by an act of our carelessness than by a wildfire. From poorly placed rags and overburdened fuses, to flying sparks during construction and clearing, humans

CHAPTER 5

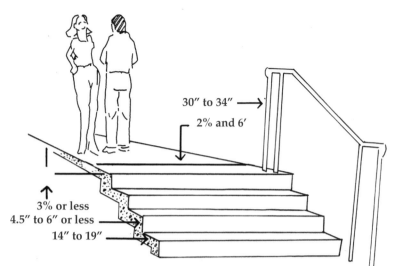

30" to 34"

2% and 6'

3% or less
4.5" to 6" or less
14" to 19"

Above are the standard guidelines landscape architects use to design steps, handrails, and paths. *Source:* Landscape Architect's Portable Handbook, *by Nicholas Dines and Kyle Brown.*

are a natural source of friction and fire. Ignition areas include garages, driveways, roadways, workspaces, outdoor dining and barbecue patios, and outhouses with engines, like well-water pumps. The garden around these ignition areas should be planted with zone 2 recommended plants.

Healthy Foundation

The foundation planting—the dominant, larger trees and shrubs of a landscape—has a large effect on the health of an entire garden. By keeping the foundation healthy, we can keep the entire garden healthy. Watering systems and maintenance budgets should be designed to sustain the foundation's health. During water shortages, a landscape's foundation should be maintained at the expense of shorter-lived shrubs, perennials, and annuals, which might have to be removed.

Islands, Not Lines

A fire-wise design will use planted islands to perform the same functions as a continuous line of plants, which is not as fire safe. Isolated groupings can screen for privacy, take the punch out of cold northerly winds, and, when used cleverly, define spaces, provide structure, and add interest to any unique landscape.

Patient Planting

Some landscapes are densely planted to create the illusion of maturity and depth. While aesthetically pleasing, such overplanted landscapes produce continuous lines of plant fuels, raise the maintenance requirements of a landscape, and promote structurally dependent plants, which rely on surrounding plants to stay upright and are prone to storm damage. A patiently planted landscape will help keep plant fuels isolated and reduce the costs of watering, removal, and maintenance.

Barriers

Planted barriers can serve a variety of needed functions in a landscape. Shrubs can block unwanted views and animals. Ground covers can help keep unwanted seeds out and much-needed topsoil in. Strategically placed trees and shrubs can protect living areas from cold winds and from pollutants that blow in from streets. Well-maintained barrier plantings can also diminish the force of wind, suck heat from the air, and catch flying sparks during a wildfire.

The 5-gallon cypress trees along this fence were planted too close together. In three years, these trees will require frequent pruning to keep them contained within the bed. In seven to 10 years, these trees' interiors will be full of bare growth, with the new growth restricted at the growing tips. In an effort to enhance privacy, the owners of this property have created a situation that will become highly flammable in the future. If the homeowners want the privacy without the fuel, they will have to thin this bed every two to three years, removing trees until the growing tips are just barely touching at maturity.

CPR

Every landscape is able to produce water runoff. In California, this tainted and unhealthy water makes it to our watersheds, groundwater supplies, ocean, and native landscapes. CPR stands for conservation, permeability, and retention—the three pillars of keeping water on a property. In a firescaped garden, water retention not only saves water and stretches a water budget, it prevents the nutrient-rich runoff from entering neighboring landscapes and increasing their plant fuels.

Continual Removal and Replanting

Removing plants is not a design element, it is simply a good idea. Everything has a life cycle. As a plant ages, the ratio of its deadwood to live wood rises. By continually removing and replanting plants, you ensure a healthy, fire-retardant garden. This practice also creates a diversity of plant ages; it helps control infestations; it reduces the impact of environmental influences, such as wind, freeze, and drought; and it staggers the ignition timing of a landscape—all the things a naturally occurring fire would do.

Designs for Special Situations

Although ideally suited for native and fire-prone landscapes, firescaping's zone theory is tough to apply to many common situations in California. Individuals living on small properties will find that there is not enough space to include all the elements of the theory. Residents under a canopy of trees can use only a small percentage of the plant list. The following designs will help you firescape the four most common problematic scenarios: slopes, ridgetops, small lots, and understory landscapes.

Slopes

Compared to fires on flat ground, fires on slopes burn hotter, run faster, and produce longer flames. For every 10 percent increase in slope, the length of flame doubles. For instance, if a shrubby-ground fire produces 5-foot-long flames, they will grow to 15 feet on a 30 percent slope, which is high enough to get into most trees.

Although the basic elements of a protected hillside home are covered below, suggestions are provided

---

Perspectives: Michael McKay, Principal of McKay Architecture, Berkeley

My wife and I live in the Berkeley Hills, north of campus. The area we're in lost a number of houses during the 1923 fire, including some notable buildings by Bernard Maybeck, well known for his contributions to the Bay Regional style of architecture. After the fire, Maybeck experimented with various types of fire-resistive construction. He built a few all-concrete buildings, switched to metal windows sash, and even tried a type of wall shingle made of gunnysacks dipped in concrete.

In terms of fire prevention now, probably the most important thing we've done was to remove some trees, including six huge eucalyptus trees that constantly dropped debris. Although they were on our neighbor's property, they were nearest to our house. We had significant debates and negotiations to get them removed; it was a lengthy process, and we ended up covering most of the expense. We also coordinate weed-whacking and brush control with our neighbors. Because of the steepness of the hillside, we don't have fences. In a dense residential area, you *have* to work with your neighbors to keep accumulated brush to a minimum. We make it a policy to know at least all our immediate neighbors by name, and have their phone numbers. Some have even become good friends in the process.

---

throughout this book to overcome the difficulties and hazards of working on slopes. Tips for performing work on slopes are in Chapter 6. Plants that help control erosion are listed in Chapter 7. Watering systems and sprinkler head placement for slopes are detailed in Chapter 8. And recommendations for temporarily controlling erosion on slopes are covered in Chapter 10.

To reduce flame lengths on slopes, the fuel break is extended proportionally to the percent of incline. For every 10 percent increase in slope, 10 feet need to be added to zone 2. For example, if a house is on a 15 percent slope, the amount of feet added to the greenbelt is 15, and the fuel break will extend 85 feet from a structure.

Keeping the area immediately around a house clear of ignitable plants and debris is as important as clearing downhill. The heat that fires produce on slopes is

These three houses, although designed differently, provide good defenses against a grass fire. The owners of the house on the left have planted a hedge that will block flying sparks and heat, and they have mowed the grass 15 feet past their fence. The house in the middle has its grass mowed 40 feet below the structure. The house on the right has low-growing shrubs to deflect wind, grass seed, and potential sparks. All three houses have skirts on their overhangs.

Amout of Defensible Space Needed: Slope vs. Vegetation			
Type of Landscape	**Steepness of Slope**		
	0–20%	21–40%	41% +
Grass, weeds, and scattered shrubs	30 ft.	100 ft.	100 ft.
Shrubs	100 ft.	200 ft.	200 ft.
Trees with little or no understory	30 ft.	100 ft.	200 ft.

Source: Home Landscaping Guide for Lake Tahoe and Vicinity, *University of Nevada Cooperative Extension, 2001.*

intense and can ignite plants and houses 100 feet away. Wood piles and compost bins should always be up-slope from a house.

The distance between the canopies of trees will influence a fire's rate of spread and its intensity. A canopy fire is an awesome sight and the hardest type to battle. The guidelines that follow on distances between canopies can be used throughout the state.

Terracing a slope has benefits. It shortens a slope's length, which reduces a fire's speed and flame length. Placed perpendicular to a slope, rock or wood walls can slow the swift winds that run uphill. Terracing also slows erosion and increases soil fertility, which increases the amount of plants that can be successfully grown. Leveled areas along a slope are also easier to maintain. However, most terraces are created using cut-and-fill construction (where a cut is made into a slope to create a pad, and the dug-up dirt is placed downhill of the pad to extend it), and this disturbs a soil's profile, making it more likely to slip. Any effort aimed at reducing the cut and fill is wise. The plants in the terraced areas will eventually anchor the beds to the slope.

The more paths a property has, the better. Clearing paths for people to get to, through, and off a landscape is as important for emergencies as it is for maintenance. Creating three ways off a landscape is preferred for large hillside properties; two ways is essential.

While any effort aimed at stopping erosion is well spent, these efforts can add a lot of fuel to a hill. Ground covers that crawl along the top of the soil are the best at slowing erosion. Deep-rooted shrubs are good at holding soils together, pulling water from saturated soils, and buffering the effects of wind and rain, but they do not control erosion as well as ground covers. No more than one deep-rooted shrub, such as huckleberry, oak, and toyon, should be

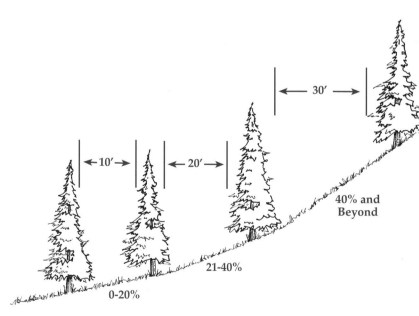

Trees should be spaced far enough apart to minimize the chance of a canopy fire. *Source: Adapted from* Home Landscaping Guide for Lake Tahoe and Vicinity, *University of Nevada Cooperative Extension, 2001.*

The people in this highly flammable neighborhood have designed a usable and less fire-prone space. Terracing allows a greater range of plants to be grown in the rocky soil, and makes it easier to maintain and enjoy the landscape, all of which lowers its flammability.

planted every 20 square feet. Be sure to surround the shrub with soil-hugging plants, such as low artemisia, ceanothus, cotoneaster, and manzanita.

Ridgetops

Properties along the top of a slope are among the most at risk for destruction. Fire can come in from any direction. The growing conditions are tough. The topsoil is constantly being blown away. The extremes of heat, cold, wind, and water have their greatest impact on ridgetops. The plants grown with success in these tough environments are typically the most flammable, like grasses, sages, and conifers.

Just like the growing conditions, people living on ridgetops must be tough. In an emergency they may be asked to play a pivotal role in battling a blaze that threatens the community beyond. But unfortunately, they must not expect to receive help from community resources, namely water and power, for these resources are commonly found below. Ridgetop homes and gardens are the most independent.

If the local fire agencies have designated a particular ridgetop as a place to fight a fire, they may be strict about enforcing local fire codes. When an emergency strikes, the area must safely aid the personnel. A well-maintained landscape will help not only the firefighters, but also the residents the firefighters are trying to save.

The owners of this ridgetop home have taken many wise steps to defend their house against a wildfire and to attract firefighters. An irrigated pasture surrounds the house, and there are no fuel ladders (such as shrubs) that would lead a ground fire into the pines, which have been immaculately maintained. There is plenty of parking, and the vegetation is cleared on either side of the road.

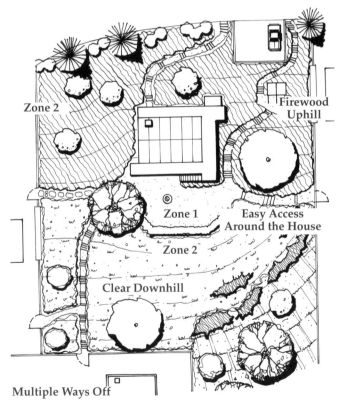

The elements of a fire-safe hillside garden are illustrated above. In this design, paths run throughout the property, providing several ways to get on and off. Neighbors are screened with a combination of low-fuel fences, the compost and firewood storage areas are placed uphill of the house, and the slope below the house is maintained with low-growing plants.

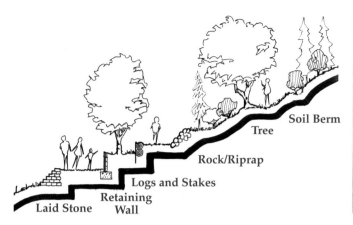

Terracing is an excellent way to lower the flammability of a hillside. It helps the hill hold more water and nutrients, while allowing easier access.

Aged and densely planted vegetation adds unnecessary risk to this house on a small, wooded lot. The pursuit of privacy has led to an excess of plant fuels while severely restricting emergency access. The house is barely visible, yet it is only 10 feet beyond the fence.

All tools used to protect a house on a hill are also used on ridgetops, but they should be implemented on all sides: large fuel breaks, easy access around the property, and regular maintenance.

Terracing is the most common method used to increase the range of plants grown in these tough conditions. Terracing varies in size, from engineered walls to a small group of rocks holding just enough soil to get a ground cover started. Slowing the movement of water and nutrients, terracing is as good for plant health as it is for fire protection.

Flammable plants can be maintained in a manner that aids emergency efforts. Whether for a single property or a cluster of homes, a large area for trucks to park and turn around must be created and maintained. Fuels around the roads and parking areas should be kept to an absolute minimum.

A house on a ridgetop might completely lose water and power services during an emergency. A water tank, an electricity generator, a water pump, and fire hoses may be the necessities of living in a perched environment. See the emergency water section in Chapter 8 for details.

Small Properties

Oakland, Berkeley, Los Angeles, and Laguna Beach have all experienced fires that defied traditional boundaries—fires that have made the leap from mountainous terrain to city streets. Many older, densely populated areas possess an incredible amount of fuel and risk.

Small lots are especially flammable for a variety of reasons. Many properties lack the room for a greenbelt, much less a highly functional yard. As the housing density increases, so do the many elements that contribute to a higher risk of fire. Privacy plantings, fences, stored wood, and ignitable debris increase as the distance between houses decreases. This unusually high density of fuel leads a fire from house to house.

Older communities are more prone to fires than newer developments. Not only do older homes typically have wood-shake roofs, but the vegetation surrounding the houses are mature, possessing a lot more ignitable leaves and branches, as was the case in the fires mentioned above.

Homeowners on small lots and in dense developments often will have to collaborate to defend themselves from wind-blown embers and intense heat. Installing a fire-retardant roof is possibly the best way to protect a structure from a wildfire. The second best way is to remove all dead, dying, and diseased vegetation from a property. Plants selected for small lots should be zone 1 or 2 plants, which are the most fire retardant. Most small lots have more water available per square foot than larger lots, and they can sustain high-moisture, fire-retardant plants. With continuous imports of water, nutrients, and maintenance time, almost any plant can be maintained so it is less flammable.

Neighbors should work together by sharing vegetation and creating access between houses. One large tree can

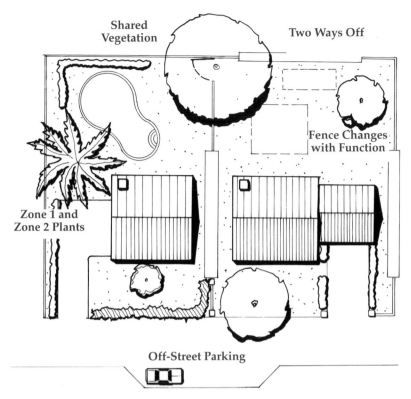

Shared Vegetation

Two Ways Off

Fence Changes with Function

Zone 1 and Zone 2 Plants

Off-Street Parking

The illustration above shows many of the elements needed for fire protection on small sites. Off-road parking, shared vegetation, and access between homes are the ingredients to success when mixed with gardens free of flammable debris. In densely packed neighborhoods, structure loss is commonly caused by firebrands landing on the roof and garden—a Class A roof is absolutely necessary.

easily provide the shade requirements for two or more houses. Sharing the benefits and maintenance costs of a large tree will create a tree that is healthy, strong, and highly functional. Fences should have gates installed so neighbors can move between properties. These fences should also be clear of ignitable vegetation. (See pages 50–52 for more details on fences.)

During a crisis, gridlock is common in high-density neighborhoods. Emergency vehicles compete with exiting cars, bringing travel in both directions to a near stop. Houses on small lots should create off-street parking to allow two-way traffic, even at the expense of yard space. Vegetation along the shoulder of a road should be ground covers. Overhanging branches should be pruned 16 feet above a road, helping to create an effective firebreak.

And lastly, fire doesn't stop at the property line. A landscape on a small lot might be only as fire retardant as the one next to it. Personal safety may require extensive public relations and negotiations with neighbors. If a neighbor threatens others with apathy and inaction, safety may also require the willingness to do the work yourself.

Understory Homes

Living under a canopy of trees is beautiful. Noises are muted, the scents are intoxicating, and the vegetation flourishes. Despite their high moisture content and lower ignitability, understory landscapes can be dangerous because they possess an enormous amount of plant fuels.

Understory environments are commonly found on valley floors, on the cool sides of hills and mountains, and in old neighborhoods lush with mature trees. Cypress, eucalyptus, fir, oak, pine, redwood, and even palms will have people comfortably living under them.

There are two common types of understory landscapes: those with no understory plants, and those with an abundance of plants growing below the trees. In high-density groves, tree litter can become incredibly thick. Trees, such as red gum eucalyptus, pine, and redwood, produce a lot of litter that inhibits ground covers from growing, restricts access, and produces the ideal conditions for a ground fire.

Pruning Danger Away

From simple inconvenience to downed power lines and extensive property damage, falling branches are a genuine concern for people living in wooded environments. In some cases, the likelihood of fracture is visible before the actual break. Simple inspection is the key. If any of the branches exhibit the following characteristics, prune or support the branch to remove the risk of a break:

- **Branch unions are tight and V-shaped.**
- **Limbs are excessively long and horizontal.**
- **There are shelf fungi or other signs of decay.**
- **Cracks have developed at the branch unions.**
- **Excessive mistletoe is growing on a branch.**

There are a lot of dangerous elements shown in this picture. Tree litter covers the roofs and ground. The houses are built close together, separated by wooden fences. Ivy is growing up the telephone poles and trees, creating fuel pathways and ladders that tie all the vegetation together. Also, the road will not accommodate two-way traffic, which is typical in canyon bottoms.

On the other hand, there are many other types of trees that are compatible with a wide range of plants growing below them. Large, understory shrubs, such as the tan bark oak and California bay, get awkwardly tall as they reach for the sun under cypress, firs, and oaks. Underneath the shrubs may be perennials, such as iris and fern. Vines—for instance, ivy and poison oak—are also common under trees, and can scramble up shrubs, trees, and telephone poles. If a fire is hot enough to ignite either of the two understory landscapes, it may be difficult, if impossible, to extinguish.

Homes under a grove of trees have to defend themselves from canopy fires, which leap from tree to tree, showering sparks and igniting everything below them, as well as ground fires, which are fueled by a grove's litter. The more fire-suppressed understory landscapes are, the greater their plant fuels and risk of fire.

Fire is only one of several dangers of understory living. Falling trees and branches are a serious threat to the people, homes, cars, and animals beneath them. Winter storms are hazardous, causing everything from auto collisions and road closures to power outages and windstorm damage. You should take care to identify and remove limbs and trees that are likely to cause problems. As a rule, an arborist should make safety recommendations every two years in dense, understory landscapes. See Chapter 9 for more information.

To make an understory landscape less flammable and safer to live in, create a landscape design and mainte-nance program that makes the garden around a home look as clear as a campground. Typical campgrounds have little deadwood, the tree litter has been walked on to the point where it lacks the oxygen to readily ignite, and there is a lot of space between understory shrubs.

Thirty feet of defensible space has to be maintained around all structures. Plants from zones 1 and 2 are recommended to protect a house from the intense heat and flying sparks. Many shade-loving and water-needy plants, such as ferns, camellias, and huckleberry, require little supplemental water in understory landscapes.

Due to the high amount of plant litter and moisture on an understory property, maintaining swift and safe access is an ongoing task. After a week of winds, paths will be cluttered with leaves and twigs. Moss grows on concrete, rock, and wood paths. Scrubbing the pathways with a weak solution of bleach and water will keep them from becoming dangerously slippery. Wood features, such as steps, stairs, and handrails, are prone to rot. Homeowners should expect higher replacement costs of wooden features in an understory environment.

And of course, do your part to prevent fires. Spark arresters should be put on all chimneys and small engines. Tree limbs should be removed to 10 feet past all chimneys and stove pipes, and to 16 feet above barbecues, fire pits, and work areas.

The health of the grove should be continually maintained. Digging and trenching should always be avoided

The understory property pictured above has many favorable characteristics. An open campground look has been designed. The driveway (an ignitable friction area) is cleared of overhanging branches. Understory shrubs, such as bay, have been removed and replaced with ferns. There are no fuel ladders that would lead a ground fire into the trees.

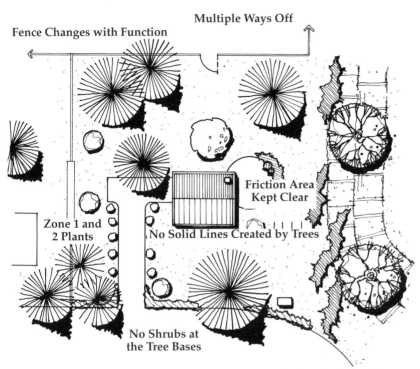

Fence Changes with Function

Multiple Ways Off

Friction Area Kept Clear

Zone 1 and 2 Plants

No Solid Lines Created by Trees

No Shrubs at the Tree Bases

The illustration above highlights some of the characteristics of a defensible understory landscape. Overhanging branches have been removed from above the patio and work area. There are no shrubs at the base of the trees' trunks. The grove has been thinned to create structurally strong trees.

within a shrub's or tree's drip line. Dirt should never be piled around the base of a tree's trunk, so as to prevent root and crown rot. Watering the plants under trees should be done carefully because overwatering can lead to oak root fungus and other damaging pathogens and pests. Trees, such as oaks, can be easily overwatered. Ideally, a tree's branches should be 10 feet away from the adjacent tree's branches. Not only does spacing help slow a fire, it aids in the tree's health. An independent tree will grow structurally stronger than trees that have grown intertwined with one another.

Landscape Features: Design and Construction Materials

A fire in California is not considered bad if it only consumed some outbuildings and fences. But any outbuildings or fences destroyed are bad because these objects caught, sustained, and, most likely, propelled the fire. These landscape features brought a fire closer to someone's home.

More often than not, our landscape features add to the buildup of fuels on a landscape, raising the flammability of a site. Below are design and construction ideas that can lower the amount of risk the features add to a landscape.

Outbuildings and Garden Sheds

Outbuildings, such as well houses and garden sheds, contribute a lot of fuel to a landscape. An outbuilding, like a house, can be designed and built to withstand wildfires. Although the elements of a less flammable structure are covered below, greater detail is provided in Chapter 4.

Roofs have the greatest influence a structure's chance of survival during a wildfire. Class A roofs have the highest fire-resistance rating, followed by B, and then C. Caution should be used when buying shake roofs that are advertised as having fire-retardant chemicals. Chemical retardants lose their effectiveness within five years, and they are not approved by fire marshals.

Other characteristics that influence a roof's ability to retard a fire are its pitch and eaves. The steeper a roof, the more flying embers it will catch. A roof should be only slightly slanted, with its pitch going in the direction of the slope. Eaves are the areas where the roof extends past the house and trap flying embers and heat. Eaves should be eliminated, boxed in with plywood, or have their undersides coated with a nonflammable material, such as plaster or stucco. Importantly, the line of a roof should never extend over a slope, because it can create erosion problems.

Overhangs are the areas of a structure that jut out over a slope and trap heat and wind-blown sparks. Examples include the undersides of decks, balconies, and structures built on stilts. Overhangs should be skirted in with plywood, drywall, or metal sheeting, or they should be screened with quarter-inch wire mesh. If overhangs cannot be skirted, their undersides should

These two drawings illustrate what less flammable outbuildings may look like.

flammable as the effects of neglect and weather accumulate, ultimately adding a lot of fuel to a landscape.

However, shelters, planters, and furniture are needed in the garden. They invite the use of a landscape, and the more an area is used, the lower its flammability. To offset their combustible nature, garden features should be made of nonflammable materials and they should be well maintained.

Proper materials are critical to any construction project. Nonflammable materials should always be used when a budget allows. Iron, steel, bricks, concrete, rocks, and tile are excellent materials. When wood is used, oversized lumber with at least a one-hour fire-resistance rating should be used. If the added expense of the suggestions above is not feasible, yet the goal for fire safety remains, the tradeoff is an increase in maintenance time. It is notable to mention that nonflammable materials extend the life of a feature, and can, in the long run, save maintenance time and replacement money.

Garden features concentrate a lot of fuel within a small area. Shade structures and arbors are examples of deadwood covered with woody vines. Using zone 1 and 2 recommended plants around garden features makes them harder to ignite. The landscape around garden features should also be well maintained.

Fences

Used with unparalleled frequency, fences have a wide variety of purposes in a garden. Fences act as barriers to people peering into living spaces; block or mute sound; keep unwanted people, pests, and things out of the garden; and make physical distinctions between proper-

This inexpensive barrier to entry shown above will eventually become a visual barrier as the vine grows, without the excess fuels. Notice the fence posts: They are larger than necessary and will be slow to ignite during a wildfire.

be coated with nonflammable material, such as plaster, stucco, concrete, or tile.

A fire-protected outbuilding has external support beams built with oversized lumber—6-by-6 inch is preferred, as it takes longer for fire to ignite such thick wood. The structure's siding should be nonflammable, like metal sheeting, or, if wood is used, the siding should be put together so there are no cracks or fissures. The windows in these small structures should be small, helping to stop the interior from igniting by conduction. As with all structures, 30 feet of defensible space should be maintained around an outbuilding.

Shelters, Planters, and Furniture

Almost every garden has unique features that add structure and interest. Shade structures, patios, benches, arbors, and planter boxes are elements that people enjoy. Over time, however, these features age and become

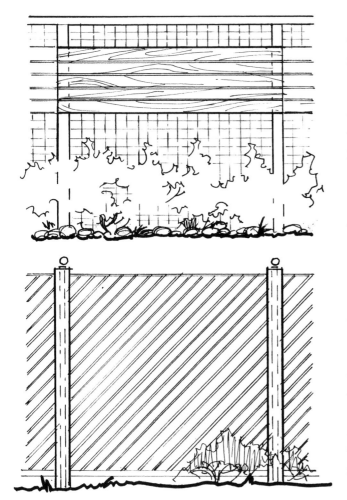

A less flammable fence restricts the use of flammable materials. The bottom drawing is a physical barrier made of metal. The upper is designed to be a visual and physical barrier.

ties. For all these reasons, fences will continue to be a dominant feature in landscapes.

Unfortunately, fences contribute an enormous amount of fuel to a garden and neighborhood. Cheap and ignitable woods are common building materials. Even nonflammable fences increase the fire risk because of the tendency to plant on both sides of them. These plantings are commonly used to hide a fence, to aid in its function as a screen, or to simply support a favored plant. An aged and overgrown fence is dangerous to the property it was designed to protect. As the distance between houses becomes smaller, the amount of fuel that fences contribute to a neighborhood increases.

Like any garden feature, the goal for a fence is to serve its unique function while resisting fire. Meeting these criteria requires identifying the specific role of a

fence, then restricting the flammable material to serve that function. This might mean you build fences that do not have to be hidden by plants, or design a fence that incorporates the use of plants.

There are four basic functions of fences, and each, in varying degrees, can be flammable and unsafe. However, you can achieve your fence's desired effect and ensure fire resistance by following these suggestions.

Visual Barrier: This is the most flammable type of fence. The visual barrier's goal is to keep wandering eyes out of an area. Overcoming the inherent flammability of this fence requires isolating the wood to the areas that screen view; the wood does not have to run to the ground or along the fence's entire length. Building the fence as close to people or areas that are trying to be screened also lowers the amount of fuel. The closer the screen is to the viewer, the more the view will be blocked.

Sound Barrier: This is the most expensive type of fence. The best barriers to sound are made from non-flammable materials, such as concrete, stucco, decorative blocks, and bricks.

Barrier to Entry: This can be the least flammable and cheapest of all fences. Chain-link fences and strong wire mesh stretched between 4- by 4-inch posts are the most effective physical barriers.

Aesthetic Divisions: These are the fences that are typically ornamental and signify a property line or a transition point in a landscape. Rocks, bricks, and large

This fence restricts flammable material by reducing the amount of wood in the fence.

This physical and visual barrier is an excellent example of a low-cost and low-flammability fence. Keeping the bottom of the fence clear of shrubs increases the air circulation and improves the health of the vine.

lumber (ranch style) are ideal materials for creating a beautiful border.

All types of conventional fences, regardless of function, create a wind eddy on the back, or lee, side of them. The wind eddy will take flying embers and deposit them off the backside of fences, igniting any material lying there or igniting the fence itself. To reduce the risk, keep the back side of the fence clear of flammable material, or install a wind-baffling device at the top of the fence. The wind baffler sends the hot wind and flying sparks up and over the fence.

Hedges

Almost as common as fences, hedges serve all the same functions and are nearly as effective. However, hedges also have many traits that can make them a dangerous element within a fire-prone community.

Hedges are continuous lines of fuel and can lead a fire throughout a garden. Because hedge plants are grown close together and sheared, they tend to have dead, twiggy interiors, with their growth, which is usually hard and small, isolated at the very tips of branches. Hedges can take many years to fill in, so gardeners are often reluctant to remove parts of these plants, even when the hedges become old, brittle, and quick to ignite.

Maintaining a safer hedge is not difficult. Every two years, 10 percent of the branches on a hedge plant should be removed to the trunk, allowing sunlight to penetrate the plant's interior, encouraging large, fleshy growth from within. Expect to replace a hedge every 20 years. The plants used for hedges should be zone 1 or 2 recommended shrubs or small trees. If a landscape has the room, a screen can be provided by plants, but the planting pattern should be staggered instead of continuous.

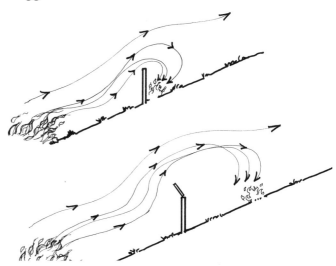

These illustrations show the wind's effect on a conventional fence (above) and on one with a baffling device (below).

Trial and Error

We often must make mistakes to create beautiful and healthy landscapes. In *52 Weeks in the California Garden* (Los Angeles Times Books, 1996), author Robert Smaus interviewed some of the most notable plant professionals in southern California and asked them to recount their biggest gardening errors. From not reading labels to planting much too deep, they admit to making some of the very same mistakes novice gardeners do.

Through these interviews, and his 25 years as the garden editor of the *Los Angeles Times*, Smaus summarized his experiences with the list below. And as it turns out, his advice is as useful for creating a beautiful garden as it is for fire protection. Landscaping for fire protection is intimately tied to plant health, and health is tied to beauty.

- Spend time preparing the soil.
- Don't plant too much.
- Beware of fast-growing plants.
- Keep on top of weeding.
- Plant at the proper depth.
- Give plants room.
- Learn how to prune properly.
- Read all labels carefully!

Chapter 6

Removing Plants and Reclaiming Landscapes

Dust flies, dirt fills your pores, and unknown muscles ache: Weeding is the hardest and least glamorous work in a garden. Although this dirty chore is often pushed aside, it is vital in creating a fire-safe and healthy garden.

Clearing plants in a firescaped garden breaks up dense concentrations of fuel. It keeps fire away from homes and out of trees. It diminishes bug and disease infestations and lowers a landscape's amount of deadwood. Removing plants is simply necessary in domestic and natural landscapes.

All organisms go through a process of birth, growth, maturity, death, and decay. As a plant matures, it becomes more flammable, slowly creating more deadwood than live. When a landscape starts displaying the signs of age, it opens the door to change.

Wildfires, winter storms, floods, pests, and even weeds are agents of change in native landscapes, clearing an aged landscape and helping start a new succession of plants. In domestic landscapes, the processes are the same, but the gardener is the agent of change. Removing aged and weakened plants—and then replanting—continues a landscape's succession, without the destructive unpredictability of nature.

As discussed in Chapter 3, people are generally reluctant to remove vegetation for reasons of privacy, preferences, difficulty, and costs, despite the known risk of fire. However, a program of regular removal is cost effective. Unhealthy or aged plants are more susceptible to damage during environmental extremes, such as freeze, fire, and wind. The costs associated with these reactionary situations are much higher than the cost to remove the plant before it becomes a threat. Plant removal is more expensive every year you put it off, as the amount of work needed to clear the vegetation increases.

Moreover, dense vegetation promotes the rapid spread of fire. Breaking up continuous lines of plant fuel and creating planted islands requires frequent removal. Crowded conditions also create poor plant health. Structurally dependent plants, which are found in densely planted areas, are more prone to storm damage. Bugs and mildew are attracted to areas with low air

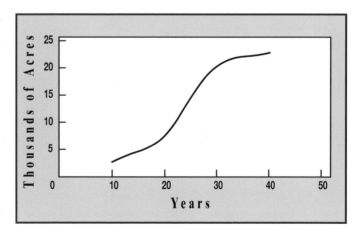

Chamise, one of the chaparral's most explosive plants, is used above to illustrate how plant age is related to severity of fire. As the age of chamise increases, so does the number of acres burned during a wildfire. Young plants are simply less flammable.

Source: Protecting Residences from Wildfire: A Guide for Homeowners, Lawmakers and Planners, *by Howard E. Moore (US Forest Service, Pacific Southwest, May 1981).*

circulation and high moisture. These pests, along with weeds, also add a lot of unwanted fuel to a garden. The longer these pests persist, the larger the unwanted infestation will grow, migrating to other plants and areas.

Plant Life Expectancy

As a landscape approaches or exceeds its natural life span, the risk of fire dramatically rises. A mature landscape is more flammable than a juvenile one. Young and rapidly growing plants and landscapes have growth and limbs that are moist, supple, and low in fuels. Use the generalized table below to budget and plan for the removal of mature plants. As illustrated, a garden that was planted 50 years ago may require the removal of some, if not most, of its plants.

Plant Group	Life Expectancy
Large trees	70–120 years
Medium trees	50–80 years
Large shrubs	20–30 years
Small shrubs	14–20 years
Vines	8–15 (except those that reproduce by root divisions)
Perennials	3–7 years
Annuals	1 year

An old and/or unhealthy plant will display the following telltale signs:

- **Older leaves, stems, and limbs are dead. On trees, 50 percent or more of the trunk have either dead limbs or no limbs.**
- **The living foliage is at the very end of the branches, instead of throughout the entire branch.**
- **During summer, the plant drops more leaves than usual.**
- **The amount of living wood is less than 50 percent of the entire plant.**
- **A bud or disease infestation is difficult, if not impossible, to control.**
- **A plant does not, or is slow to, recover from injury.**
- **A plant is showing signs of decay, which could include mushrooms coming up from its base and roots, or shelf fungi along its trunk.**

This false cypress is old and highly ignitable. Its interior is loaded with dead, twiggy wood, and the growth is isolated at the end of the branches. This plant should be removed.

General Guidelines for Removal and Reclamation

Removing large areas of vegetation may not be a one-time event. The initial clearing may be a temporary solution to a recurring problem. In these difficult-to-control situations, a maintenance program will be needed to reclaim the landscape. A landscape cleared but not reclaimed can quickly reestablish itself in two to five years.

Reclaiming a landscape from unwanted plants is a lengthy process. Reclamation may involve many months of diligent weeding, patiently exhausting the soil of its stored seeds. It might require putting up barriers or weeding a neighbor's yard, slowing the migration of seeds. In most situations, reclamation

Perspectives: Jan Brisco, Executive Director, Tahoe Lakefront Owners' Association

I think everybody [here] is extremely concerned [with the risk of wildfire]. It is not a question of if, but when, especially on the west side, which is very steep, very dense forest. But we're not doing enough in our neighborhoods, and in our particular communities, to organize. A lot of people think that you don't have to maintain anything: This is the natural setting, and you just let everything go. Some people don't want to spend the money or take the time to do it. And not everybody thinks about pine needles accumulating on their roofs.

The whole Tahoe basin was essentially clear-cut at the turn of the century, and much of what has come back and been replanted are nonindigenous species, such as the white fir and lodgepole pine, because they were rapid growing. The problem with the lodgepole is that they grow very close together and, of course, very straight. We've got massive forests, where probably only the top one-third is actually growing; the bottom two-thirds is all the dead and dying limbs that can't get enough [sun] to grow. It makes for a very precarious fuels issue.

I would try to motivate homeowner associations and community outreach [to] sponsor meetings at fire stations for residents. Maybe even partner with the conservation corps or other volunteer organizations [to] actually do the work for property owners, many of whom are elderly or maybe can't afford to do it. Start at the grassroots level and let people know that they've got to help themselves, property by property.

This area was completely cleared eight months ago. A late spring rain and plenty of sun provided the ideal conditions for germinating leftover seeds. If this area is not weeded again, the scotch broom will have a chance to produce seed, extending the process of reclamation for another couple years.

Personal Safety

Clearing land is not only hard physical labor, it involves the use of dangerous equipment. Always wear eye and ear protection when using weed-whackers, chainsaws, and chippers. Ankle-high boots, thick pants, long-sleeved shirts, and gloves should be worn like a uniform.

Moderation

Trying to tackle too much at one time can lead to a variety of problems. Erosion, an invasion of weeds, storm damage, and even personal injury are common when quality is sacrificed for quantity. Never clear more than can be replanted in one season, especially on slopes. Also, stagger the removal of shrubs and trees in dense groves. If too much of the grove is taken out at one time, wind, freeze, and sun damage is likely. Selectively remove no more than 30 percent of a plant or grove at a time, planning to come back in two years to remove another 30 percent.

Equipment

According to the California Department of Forestry, the leading cause of wildfires is equipment use. The mowers, weed-whackers, and chainsaws used to clear land are constant sources of friction, heat, and sparks. To avoid starting a fire while working with machinery, be sure to take the following precautions:

will require planting and/or seeding, helping to establish a plant that can aggressively take an area from an undesired species.

One of the most important aspects of clearing or reclamation is the follow-through. Clearing an area for the first time is a stimulant to many plants and seeds. Seeds are distributed when hauling the vegetation, and the recently disturbed soil is an ideal incubator when warmed by the sun. If new sprouts from the remaining trunks and seeds are not removed before they set seed, the problem will be back next season. Plan to return to the area within two months and pull the remaining unwanted plants.

Before renting a tiller or buying herbicides, consider some general guidelines about the processes of removal and reclamation.

- **Put spark arresters on all exhaust ports, and repair holes in existing systems and arresters.**
- **Check for a buildup of carbon in exhaust systems and on spark plugs.**
- **Refuel only when the engine has cooled down.**
- **Never lay a running or hot engine in grass or other ignitable vegetation.**
- **Bring a fire extinguisher to the work site.**
- **Avoid working past 10 A.M. during the fire season.**
- **Avoid all work that involves machinery during extreme fire-weather conditions—hot, dry, windy days.**

Timing

Some people wait to clear land until a point of crisis, typically at the height of every fire season. But this can do more harm than good—it can even start a fire, as mentioned above. Late winter and early spring are the best times to clear landscapes: Most plants have only begun growing, and only a few have set seed. The soil is also easy to work. A landscape will recover more quickly when nourished by the lengthening days and gentle rains expected in mid to late spring.

Ecology

Bacteria, bugs, and plants coexist in a garden; hurt one and others suffer as well. When clearing, take great care to minimize damage to these important residents of your micro-ecosystem. Protect plants from falling and dragged debris. Lay boards and plywood over beds and grasses to help distribute the weight of repeated footsteps. If working in dry conditions, a light watering will help bind the soil, dampening the dust. Never work in soil that is soggy; it can cause compaction and degrade the health of the soil.

Herbicides

All herbicides should be well understood and used with care. More often than not, unwanted vegetation will have to be removed by hand, and killing plants prior to pulling makes the task harder.

Herbicides are available in three varieties. The first, called a nonselective herbicide, is indiscriminate and kills all plants. The most effective nonselective is a translocative or systemic herbicide. The systemic herbicide is drawn in by the plant and flows through its system, killing cells as it travels. The second class of herbicides is selective and kills only monocots (grasses) or dicots (broadleaf plants). The third class is a chemical preemergent and inhibits seeds from germinating.

Barriers

The seeds of unwanted plants can be persistent and will find a variety of ways into a garden: on wind, off cars, from birds and pets, and from tools and shoes. Wind-blown seeds are possibly the most common. To reduce the constant migration of seeds, a gardener must install barriers. There are a variety of barriers that protect a garden from wind-borne seeds. For instance, sprawling shrubs and hedges along the street trap seeds, and raised beds and planters deter them. Simply identify the landscape from where the seeds are coming from and create a barrier.

Removal Methods

Ground covers, shrubs, and trees grow and reproduce in different ways, and for that reason, there are various methods of successfully removing these types of plants.

The row of rosemary shown above helps control the grass seeds that fly in from the pasture across the street. The fine debris and seeds are visibly trapped from going farther.

From manual clearance to herbicide application to prescribed burns, you should choose the method that best suits your landscape and community needs.

Ground Covers

Ground covers, specifically grasses, are quick to ignite and quickly propel a fire. The controls for grasses and broadleaf ground covers are different, and each is described below.

Grasses

California's fire potential has increased dramatically with the introduction of annual grasses, especially the oats and barley supplied for and spread by cattle. Although grasses don't burn intensely, they can ignite an adjacent structure. Below are effective controls for aggressive annual grasses as well as difficult perennials, such as Bermuda and crabgrasses, which sprout from underground runners (called stolons).

Pulling is the best method to get rid of any plant, including grasses. This method is ideal in flat areas and with plants that have not yet set seeds (pulling sows the seeds). Pulling the stolon varieties is the most effective but also the most time-consuming way to control them. Luckily, roots exposed to sun and dry air die quickly.

If the goals of removal are to make an area look better, stop the proliferation of seeds, or lessen the fire risk, then mowing or weed-whacking is the favored approach. Plan to mow tall grasses at least twice before summer—once in early spring and again in early summer. Always rake up the grass clippings 30 feet around a house.

Tilling grasses in February and March, when the blades are green and nitrogen rich, will nourish the soil and is preferred in areas designated for replanting. Over the course of two months, the tilled grass will decompose, the upturned soil will settle, and the number of new shoots will dwindle. Stolon varieties should only be tilled if they were either killed first, or if a 3- to 5-inch layer of mulch will be thrown over the area when finished. Watering after tilling encourages the remaining roots and seeds to sprout, which then can be pulled.

Herbicides are used with frequency to control grasses. Grass is a monocot and can be controlled with all three types of herbicides. The most effective herbicide is nonselective and systemic. A selective herbicide is used to kill grasses that grow around broadleaf plants, but may require more than one application.

Mulching is a soil-enriching control that deters seeds from sprouting by blanketing and robbing them of needed oxygen and sunlight. However, too little mulch may promote growth by providing moisture, even temperatures, and nourishment to the remaining seeds or shoots. A layer of mulch 3 to 5 inches is an effective weed deterrent.

In general, grass is excellent for composting, adding needed moisture and nitrogen. However, stolon varieties, seeds, and diseased vegetation should never be put into a compost pile, because they may resurface or re-infect the garden.

Broadleaf

Ivy, bramble (berries), honeysuckle, and poison oak are a few of the sprawling plants that can pose a substantial fire risk. Because many soft, wooded ground covers grow from broken roots and branches, getting rid of them can be difficult.

Pulling broadleaf ground covers requires a lot of tools and muscle. Clippers, picks, and shovels make the job easier. Missed roots and branches are unavoidable. Watering directly after pulling encourages the roots, branches, and seeds left behind to sprout, which then can be pulled, exhausting the soil of stored weeds.

Tilling can be an exercise in futility and frustration. A powerful tiller can be used after the surface growth has been removed. Tilling only the remaining roots will, hopefully, expose and kill them. Poison oak should never be tilled.

Herbicides of the selective type are available to kill only broadleaf plants. However, the most effective chemical control is the nonselective, translocative type.

Spraying large areas with herbicides, without removing any vegetation, may seem easy, but it can create an even larger fire hazard once the landscape has died. The dead vegetation still has to be removed by hand, but

Something to Chew On

Vegetation management is a problem that gnaws at people's pocketbooks. Cows, goats, sheep, and even llamas have been called up throughout California to take a bite out of this problem.

Grass-eating cows have been successfully reducing the fire risk in the East Bay Regional Park District for many years. Eating forbs and woody brush, sheep came over with the Spanish and can be seen grazing along the levees in the Central Valley. And goats, which can devour poison oak, blackberries, and pampas grass, have been eating away at Laguna Beach's fire hazard and patience for a number of years.

Properly managed grazing can increase wildflowers and perennial grasses, along with the presence of a variety of birds and small animals. Grazing can also help restore landscapes in a state of deterioration. On the other hand, overgrazing is damaging and can lead to erosion, tainted water, and a large decrease in the landscape's productivity.

The decision to employ grazers will probably evolve from economies of scale; people managing small landscapes will find that grazers are expensive, whereas someone with five or more acres will see a better return. All professional grazers in California understand the principles of controlled and rotational grazing. If you plan to use the animals yourself, you will definitely need to know these principles. The California Grazing Academy, in Yuba County, is the state's leading school on such matters. They can be reached at (916) 889-7385.

now it is more difficult and painful (it is easier to work with supple plants rather than brittle ones). The bulk of the vegetation should be removed before applying an herbicide, and the chemical should be applied only to new shoots. If using an herbicide without removing any of the top vegetation—as would be the case with poison oak—apply it in early autumn when a plant's energy is traveling from its leaves to its roots.

Composting broadleaf ground covers is difficult. The entangled mess makes using anything less than an 8-horse-power chipper infeasible. If the material can be chipped, it typically produces woody mulch that takes a while to decompose. Although poorly suited for an active compost pile, the chipped material is ideal mulch for erosion control, weed suppression, and softening paths.

Shrubs

Shrubs enable a ground fire to leap to homes and trees. Igniting from either above or below, shrubs burn hotter and longer than grasses and broadleaf ground covers. Dense concentrations and poorly placed shrubs can be dangerous. However, many shrubs are functional and beautiful. Maintaining the functional qualities, while reducing the risk, motivates a thoughtful gardener to remove and prune shrubs.

Depending on the person, pulling requires or develops big muscles and tenacity. Removing the crown of resprouting shrubs—such as broom, bay, cotoneaster, and sumac—is the best way to control them. Prior to pulling shrubs off slopes, you should develop a follow-up plan to control topsoil loss and erosion. It is likely that a shrub is reseeding itself as it is being removed, so consider coming back and weeding.

Cutting shrubs to the ground is preferred on hills, on plants too difficult to pull, and to quickly reduce fuel. The stump and remaining roots will take between three to seven years to decompose. Be sure to cut a shrub's trunk to the ground, to minimize the chance of something or someone getting impaled. Herbicides can prevent new growth.

Herbicides have a limited role when clearing shrubs for fire safety. There is no advantage in killing shrubs without severely pruning them first. Dead vegetation is a greater fire hazard, harder to cut, tougher to chip, and more painful to remove. A nonselective, translocative

The manner in which this area was cleared poses a significant hazard to anything or anyone traveling through the landscape. The cuts were made diagonally, making this shrub and area dangerous.

herbicide should be applied only to recently cut stems and trunks of resprouting plants.

Composting shrubs is easy with a chipper that can devour 3-inch branches. Chip and compost the vegetation immediately following removal; the plants' moisture makes chipping easier and accelerates decomposition. Chipped material given directly to a garden will temporarily rob the soil of nitrogen. Adding a nitrogen supplement to the soil will compensate for this loss.

A variety of shrubs, such as bay, chamise, pittosporum, juniper, and native sages, produces resins and toxins, which naturally inhibit a competitor's growth. Although resinous plants should not be composted, they are excellent when used as a mulch to deter weeds.

Trees

Trees possess more fuel than any other type of vegetation. When they catch fire, their flames can leap hundreds of feet into the air, sending off burning embers that can ignite structures miles away. Reducing the fuel load of trees dramatically decreases your risk of a deadly conflagration.

The distance between trees affects a garden's flammability and health. Closely grown trees create more plant litter and are more prone to freeze, storm, drought, and infestation damage. When upper foliage blocks the sun, lower branches prematurely die, resulting in narrow trunks with top-heavy growth. Creating and maintaining proper distance between trees is as important to fire protection as it is to a grove's health.

Removing trees is dangerous. Consult or hire a certified arborist before felling a tree near a structure. For tips on hiring an arborist, see the pruning section in Chapter 9. Additionally, utility companies, cities, or counties can be convinced to remove or prune a tree if shown that their tree poses a risk to their interests, such as power lines, or a significant risk to your house, in which case they would have to pay for damages. Patience is needed, though; it can take a while for a request to be approved.

Pulling a tree's trunk from the ground is extremely difficult. For the most part, removing a trunk is unnecessary; only limited garden space and construction demands make this a required task. The best method is to wrap a thick chain around the trunk of the tree and

The new sprouts from this blue gum eucalyptus are less than a year old. This growth could have been prevented by slowly applying a nonselective herbicide to the stump after the tree was cut down.

pull it out using a truck, a winch, or a pulley system. If you can't do that, expect to spend three to eight hours using shovels and picks. Some trees, such as acacia, locust, poplar, and willow, will sprout from roots left behind.

Cutting down a tree, without removing its crown, is commonly done on open land and slopes. To take a stump below the soil requires a stump grinder, which should be available at equipment rental shops. Stumps and roots left in the ground take up to 15 years to decompose.

Herbicides have a limited use when removing trees. A nonselective, translocative herbicide can be used to control trees that resprout from their crown or roots,

CHAPTER 6

such as acacia, bay, eucalyptus, pine, plum, and poplar. To control a tree that sprouts after injury, make several long cuts along the area where the bark meets the heartwood and then slowly apply the herbicide to the cuts.

Recycling a tree depends on a garden's ability to absorb the vegetation. Leaves and the smallest branches can go into a compost pile; limbs and branches can be chipped and turned into a mulch; and the larger branches and trunk can be made into a border, bench, or firewood.

Most trees make decent firewood. As a rule, the lighter the wood, the faster it dries, and the more sparks it produces when on fire. For this reason, pine, cypress, and bay should not be burned in an unprotected area. Splitting wood 30 days after cutting is ideal; the milky sap is gone, but enough moisture remains to make splitting easy. Wood cures best when stacked so air can circulate throughout the pile.

A tree can make a lot of mulch. Eucalyptus, bay, cypress, pine, and the many other varieties with resins and toxins are excellent as a mulch to deter weeds.

Prescribed Burns

Although not yet widely used, prescribed burns will ultimately assume a larger role in controlling the buildup of plant fuels in California. According to a variety of experts, prescribed burns can reduce fuels by 50 percent and the damage done by wildfires by 90 percent. Agencies employing this control method set burns only in the ideal conditions, based on a formula of temperature, humidity, wind speed, topography, and fuel type.

As a method of reclamation, burning has a lot of benefits. It keeps roots intact on slopes, can take place under trees, encourages native plants in open spaces, and produces fewer pollutants, both gaseous and particulate, than a wildfire. Burning saves money, too: Mechanically cutting and removing fuel is about five times more expensive. Lastly, burning definitely reduces flammable situations, whereas as logging may not, as we are seeing in Lassen, Plumas, and Tahoe counties.

Fears and concerns about prescribed burns are legitimate. Igniting land outside of the prescription area is the greatest fear. However, only a few fires have escaped, and those that have, have done very little damage to structures. The release of hydrocarbons and volatile organic compounds is another concern for those living next to burns. To compensate for the impact on air quality, many fire agencies have begun working with local air-quality districts to extend the prescription to include weather that would divert the pollutants away from populated areas.

One of the greatest benefits of prescribed burns is to the native and fire-adapted plant communities. Many of these landscapes are in poor health or overrun by aggressive exotics. Fire stimulates these communities and begins to eradicate non-fire-adapted plants. However, for fire to reduce risk and work as a stimulant, it must be employed on a regular basis. Depending on the type of plant community, fire will be needed every 15 to 40 years.

A prescribed burn was used to provide a fuel break between natural and native landscapes, in hopes of stopping a wildfire from rushing into the housing developments on the other side of the road. Although some of the residents opposed the burn, the hill recovered swiftly and was covered in wildflowers the following spring, creating a beautiful and beneficial environment for all the communities surrounding it.

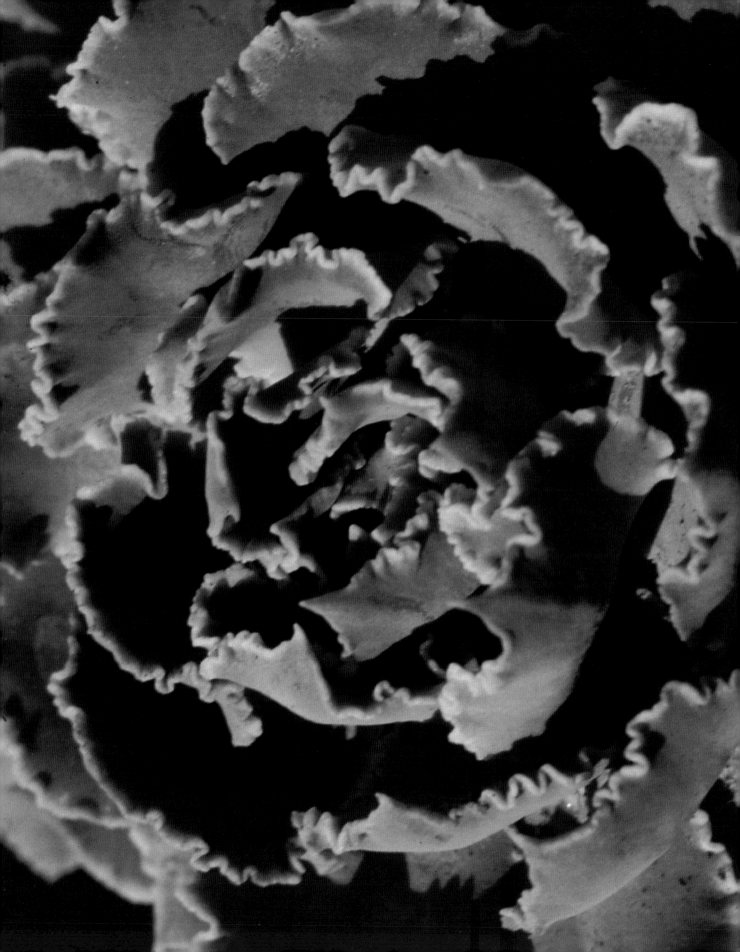

Chapter 7

Plants and Fire Prevention

Second only to roof type, the plants surrounding a house have an enormous influence in determining a home's survival during a wildfire. Vegetation will either lead a fire to a structure, or stop it.

Lawns, succulents, and rocks are recommended design ideas with impeccable records for stopping wildfires. Unfortunately, these landscaping choices do not satisfy many of the other demands placed on California gardens. Privacy, aesthetics, erosion control, and wildlife enhancement require plants of many different sizes, characteristics, and preferences.

Picking plants for a firescaped garden is tough because at one point or another, every plant will burst into flames. All of the plants recommended in this chapter can catch on fire, but they are less likely to do so than others (except for the flammable plants listed at the end). Three gauges are used to determine a plant's degree of flammability: ignitability, sustainability, and combustibility.

Ignitability is determined by counting the seconds it takes a plant to burst into flames when exposed to grass or forest fire temperatures, roughly between 650°F and 1,100°F. A plant's leaf thickness and moisture content directly affect the amount of time the plant takes to ignite. A succulent is much harder to ignite than grass, because of its thick, moisture-laden leaves.

Once a plant has burst into flames, its ability to keep the fire going determines its sustainability. The amount of fuel a plant possesses governs sustainability. A grassy landscape cannot sustain a fire like chaparral.

The amount of heat a plant is capable of producing when on fire determines its combustibility. Tissue density and chemical composition are the largest factors influencing combustibility. While an oak is harder to ignite than a pine, it will produce more heat once started. The greater the heat, the greater the likelihood that the fire will spread.

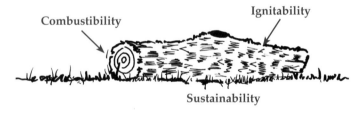

The illustration above shows the three gauges used to determine a plant's degree of flammability.

Whether a plant will catch on fire, keep a fire going, and propel a fire is determined by its physical characteristics. Getting to know these qualities is fundamentally more important than remembering plant lists. In general, the flammability of a plant is directly related to its amount of stored moisture and fuel. Ice plant (very low flammability) and pine (very high) represent the two opposite extremes. Following is a list of general plant types and how flammable they are, depending on their characteristics:

- **Deciduous plants are less flammable than evergreens.**
- **Broadleaf plants are less flammable than those with needle and bladelike leaves.**
- **Moist and easily bent leaves are less flammable than stiff and leatherlike leaves.**
- **Thick leaves are less flammable than fine or thin leaves.**

- **Plants that produce a low amount of litter are less flammable than those that produce a lot of litter.**
- **Plants with sap that looks more like water are less flammable than plants with thick, gummy, or resinous sap.**
- **Plants without fragrance are less flammable than plants with aromatic qualities.**
- **Plants with silver or gray leaves, which have a high mineral and ash content, are less flammable than those without. However, some plants, such as the highly ignitable native fragrant sages, do not follow this rule.**
- **Plant leaves without hair (cilia) are less flammable than those with hair; this also applies to the underside of leaves.**

These two pictures illustrate the inherent problems with plant lists. While the santolina, heavenly bamboo, and pancake cactus are all on the fire-wise plant lists, the plants in these pictures are far from being fire resistant or fire retardant. Maintenance truly determines a plant's ability to slow or stop a fire.

Perspectives: Ken Montgomery, ecologist, horticulturalist, and owner of Anderson Valley Nursery, Boonville

I live in rural Mendocino County, in a small town called Boonville. It's about 120 miles north of San Francisco. I've been here 27 years. [Before moving here] I was at the Los Angeles Arboretum in Arcadia. I was in charge of the fire-retardant plant project, which was part of the research division. I came and took over that project in '67 or '68, shortly after the big Bel Air fire, in which 454 homes burned in the Bel Air–Brentwood district. It was the most destructive fire anybody had seen. It was a big deal. I left the program [in 1977] for a career and lifestyle change.

Mendocino County until 10 years ago was so rural that the so-called urban/wildland interface was pretty minimal. The interface was mostly apple and pear orchards, not homes and property. But now, as Mendocino County is rapidly developing, just like elsewhere in northern California, there's a growing problem. These are many of the same issues that I remember dealing with in Arcadia and the San Gabriel Valley in the 1960s. Everybody is wringing their hands about the growing urban/wildland interface and the fire danger it presents. It's like a big cycle for me; part of my life is being replayed.

This chapter provides recommendations for plants according to specific firescaping zones, with special instructions for planting on slopes. Within each zone are the plants that are best at serving that zone's unique goals, discussed in greater detail in Chapter 4. However, most recommended plants can be used throughout a landscape. For example, if a drought-tolerant garden is being planted, then zone 2 and 3 recommended plants are practical in zone 1.

At the end of this chapter is a list of highly flammable plants. These plants are considered highly ignitable and combustible and should not be planted around a home in fire-prone communities.

Remember, every plant recommended in this chapter can catch on fire. The ability of any of these plants to retard or resist a fire depends on their condition. Any plant that is overaged, water-stressed, infested by pests, or improperly cared for is more flammable as a consequence. Truly, landscape maintenance—not plant selection—is the fulcrum of fire safety.

CHAPTER 7

Selecting Plants for Hills

Choosing plants for any degree of slope is a methodical process. The risks of fire and erosion, along with the costs of construction and maintenance, rise for every degree of a hill's incline. And plant selection affects future risks and costs. The best plants for hillsides produce little fuel, grow close to the ground, and are easy to maintain.

Plant fuels must be kept to a minimum on slopes. Avoid plants that have twiggy interiors and produce a lot of litter, like coyote brush, as well as those that easily reseed, such as pampas grass. Shrubs taller than 18 inches are not recommended unless the added height serves a specific purpose, such as screening a view.

Ground-hugging plants slow erosion. Growth that lies on top of the soil helps to keep soil particles in place and protects the soil from the effects of water, wind, and gravity. If you'd like to use shrubs as ground covers, which is common in zone 3, choose prostrate and sprawling varieties. Ground-hugging plants also suppress the growth of weeds.

Due to the difficulties and hazards of working on slopes, always select low-maintenance plants. Once established, low-maintenance plants need little or no nutrients and attention—such as pruning. They survive and thrive under the site's natural conditions: soil type, sun exposure, temperature extremes, and water availability. Low-maintenance plants also help keep foot traffic off a slope, reducing topsoil loss.

Fertile hillsides with an inch of topsoil, an irrigation system, and southeast exposure, can sustain a multitude

Nine months after a fire, the madrone shown in this picture has produced a lot of new growth, which will help decrease topsoil loss.

of low-fuel, ground-hugging, and low-maintenance plants. Hahn's ivy, periwinkle, giant inch plant, pork and beans, and gazanias are some of the many fire-retardant and fire-resistant ground covers that can be grown in such an environment. On the other hand, a slope with rocky soil, no irrigation system, and southwest exposure requires tougher plants. Varieties that grow well, resist fire, and slow erosion under these conditions include emerald green manzanita, bearberry, dwarf coyote brush, Carmel creeper, and creeping mahonia.

Another important characteristic of good plants for slopes is their ability to resprout. Resprouting plants reduce topsoil loss after a fire because they produce new growth within weeks after they have been cut or burned to the ground. Most of the plants recommended in zone 3 possess this quality. Ornamental examples include ivy, perennial grass, cotoneaster, periwinkle, oleander, myoporum, and wild ginger. In natural landscapes with no supplemental water, choose California natives: oak, ceanothus, chokeberry, sugarbush, salal, and toyon.

Although Mediterranean plants are routinely recommended on steep slopes, in some cases they may do

Prostrate ceanothus, silver spreader (Artemisia caucasica), ground morning glory (Convolvulus maurutananicus), and Pride of Madeira (Echium fastuosum) are doing an excellent job of protecting the structure from fire and holding this central California hillside.

CHAPTER 7

...ore harm than good. These drought-tolerant, deep-rooting plants can pry apart naturally occurring divisions in rock and soil. As these divisions widen, water is able to seep in and create a slick area between the two surfaces, increasing the likelihood of small rock- and mudslides. Small soil slides are common in rocky terrain and on the shoulders of slopes that have been cut to create a road or a pad for a structure. If your property's slope is prone to slides, avoid deep-rooting shrubs and trees and select fleshy, sprawling plants, such as small-leafed ivy, verbena, Santa Barbara daisy, and cape honeysuckle. Many grasses, annuals, and seeded perennials work well on slide-prone slopes and include the California brome, molate fescue, and rose clover. See Chapter 10 for a complete list of seeds used on slopes.

Recommended Plants by Zone

These lists of recommended plants for each firescaping zone are culled from firsthand observations of burned landscapes, data from field tests performed in California and the western United States, and recommendations from private and public organizations throughout California. Many experts in fire ecology, botany, and plant cultivation also offered their assistance. *Sunset Western Garden Book* was a valuable tool.

There are, however, many native and cultivated plants that did not make the cut for the purposes of this chapter. That doesn't necessarily mean that the omitted plants are unfavorable. For example, the common hackberry, *Celtis occidentalis*, and the jacaranda tree, *Jacaranda mimosifolia*, can be used in a firescaped garden, but you will not find them in the list below because they do not possess all the characteristics of a less flammable plant. In contrast, the lemon bottlebrush tree, *Callistemon citrinus*, and some melaleucas, most notably *Melaleuca armillaris* and *M. linariifolia*, have many flammable characteristics, yet they aren't regarded as high fire risks because they also possess some favorable traits. The following recommendations are the best choices as they meet both zone requirements and gardeners' desires.

Zone 1: Garden Zone

Extending 30 feet from a house, the garden zone is capable of withstanding flying embers and intense heat. Plants selected in this zone have fleshy, moist, and broad leaves. Trees are preferably deciduous. This is the only zone where plants can be dependent on water, nutrients, and labor.

Plant Characteristics Key

Deciduous.

Deer resistant. The eating habits of deer vary according to the type of landscape, the season, and environmental influences. Some of the plants recommended may be eaten by deer but have a lower likelihood than other plants. Deer dislike plants with strong odors and fine leaves, which are typically flammable plants.

Erosion controlling. A plant capable of slowing erosion protects the soil from the effects of water, wind, and gravity. An erosion-controlling plant may have one or more of the following characteristics: growth that lies on top of the soil; many surface roots; produces some, but not a lot, of litter.

Good screen or windbreak. A well-maintained screen can block wind, unwanted views, and even fire. During a fire, a planted screen can act as a barrier to flying embers and slow the speed of wind. Screens shouldn't be repeatedly sheared, as that will result in a twiggy interior that can become increasingly flammable over time.

Water thrifty. This is a relative symbol and can mean no summer water, infrequent summer water, or watering only every two weeks in summer, as in the case of many ground covers.

*spp. = Half or more of the recommended species in a genus possess the same characteristics. For example, *Geranium* spp., which is a zone 1 ground cover, means that all of the true geraniums can used as a ground cover in zone 1.

Ground Covers

Botanical Name	Common Name	Care and Habitat	Chacteristics
Agrostis spp., *Cynodon dactylon, Poa pratensis, Festuca rubra, Lolium perenne, Stenotaphrum secundatum*	Lawn grasses: bent, Bermuda, Kentucky blue, red fescue, perennial rye, St. Augustine	Grows throughout California. While they are the most expensive ground cover to maintain, lawns have an impeccable record for stopping ground fires.	
Ajuga spp.	Carpet bugle	Will freeze, but can grow anywhere with shade and water.	[deer]
Alyssum spp.	Alyssum	Not sweet alyssum (*Lobularia maritima*). Grows throughout California.	[water drop]
Asarum caudatum	Wild ginger	Can take a freeze, but not intense heat.	[deer]
Campanula spp.	Bellflower	Can tolerate a freeze, but not intense heat.	[deer]
Ceratostigma plumbaginoides	Dwarf plumbago	Grows throughout California, except in desert.	[deer] [water drop]
Chamaemelum nobile	Chamomile	Tough, good lawn substitute. Grows throughout California. Not the herb (*Matricaria recuitita*).	[deer]
Erodium reichardii	Cranesbill	Can tolerate frost, but not desert conditions. Prefers coast.	[deer]
Festuca spp.	California, sheep, red, and tall fescue	Grows throughout California.	[deer] [anchor] [water drop]
Gazania spp. hybrids (e.g., 'Aztec Queen,' 'Copper King')	Clumping gazania	Dislikes freezes and long, wet winters.	[deer]
Geranium spp.	Cranesbill	Hardy. Grows throughout California. *G. incanum* prefers mild coastal areas.	[deer]
Hedera helix, H. 'Hahn's Self Branching,' H. 'Needlepoint'	English ivy, including Hahn's and smaller-leafed varieties	Grows everywhere but high mountains and high desert.	[deer] [anchor] [water drop]
Lotus corniculatus	Bird's foot trefoil	Tolerates tough conditions. Goes dormant in extreme winters.	

CHAPTER 7

Ground Covers, cont.

Botanical Name	Common Name	Care and Habitat	Chacteristics
Pelargonium peltatum	Ivy geranium	Can hold a slope on the coast. Good performer in mild climates.	⚓
Potentilla tabernaemontanii	Potentilla, spring cinquefoil	Needs protection from extremes.	🦌
Pratia pedunculata, Laurentia fluviatilis, or more commonly, *Isotoma fluviatilis*	Blue star creeper	Grows everywhere but in desert.	🦌
Sagina subulata	Irish moss, scotch moss	Grows everywhere but in desert.	🦌
Scaevola 'Mauve Clusters'	Mauve clusters	Prefers mild, coastal climates. Dislikes temperature extremes.	🦌 💧
Tradescantia fluminensis	Wandering Jew	Aggressive in light shade and can survive freezing and any amount of heat.	🦌
Tropaeolum spp.	Nasturtium	Thrives along coast, where in some places it has naturalized.	🦌
Veronica spp.	Veronica, speedwell	Versatile enough for every garden.	🦌
Vinca spp.	Periwinkle	Grows anywhere but high elevations. *V. minor* needs more shade in hot, dry summers.	🦌
Viola odorata	Sweet violet	Prefers the mild coast. Will naturalize in wet winters.	🦌
Zoysia spp.	Zoysia	Lawn substitute. Likes a sunny summer, not freezes and long winters.	🦌

CHAPTER 7

Perennials

Botanical Name	Common Name	Care and Habitat	Characteristics
Acanthus mollis	Bear's breech	Durable plant. Grows everywhere but in snow.	🦌 💧
Agapanthus spp.	Lily-of-the-Nile	Durable everywhere but in high desert and high mountains. Somewhat deer resistant.	💧
Armeria spp.	Sea pink, thrift	Grows throughout California. Performs best by coast.	🦌
Artemisia schmidtiana	Angel's hair	Grows throughout California.	🦌 💧
Bergenia spp.	Bergenia	Tolerates everything but desert heat.	🦌 💧
Canna hybrids	Canna	A tropical best at or near the coast.	🦌
Centaurea cineraria, C. gymnocarpa	Dusty miller	A durable perennial anywhere below 2,500 feet.	🦌 💧
Chrysanthemum frutescens	Marguerite	Thrives anywhere along coast. Dislikes extremes.	🦌
Chrysanthemum maximum	Shasta daisy	A reliable performer. Grows almost everywhere.	🦌
Chrysanthemum ptarmiciflorum	Dusty miller	Perennial in marine-influenced, frost-free areas, annual elsewhere.	🦌
Coreopsis spp.	Coreopsis	Excellent color for central and southern coasts.	💧
Digitalis spp.	Foxglove	Grows as an annual throughout California. Can naturalize in woodland areas along central and northern coasts.	🦌
Erysimum 'Compact Bowles Mauve'	Wallflower	Favors the northern coast, but will grow into southern.	🦌 💧
Euryops spp.	Euryops	Prefers coasts. Dislikes deserts with a prolonged freeze.	🦌 🪟 💧
Hemerocallis spp.	Daylily	Grows easily throughout California. Tuberous and pest free.	🦌 💧
Heuchera sanguinea	Coral bells	Grows throughout California.	🦌
Hosta spp.	Hosta, plantain lily	Prefers climates with pronounced winters. Used for foliage.	🦌
Impatiens spp.	Impatiens	Prefers mild coastal climates.	🦌
Linaria purpurea	Toadflax	Grows easily throughout California.	💧

Perennials, cont.

Botanical Name	Common Name	Care and Habitat	Characteristics
Liriope spp. and *Ophiopogon* spp.	Lily turf, Mondo grass	Prefers coast.	🦌
Lychnis coronaria	Dusty miller	Grows throughout California.	🦌 💧
Malva spp.	Mallow	Grows throughout California. Short-lived.	
Pelargonium spp.	Geranium	Performs best by beach. Dislikes extremes. Dependable color.	
Penstemon gloxinioides, P. newberryi, P. pinifolius	Penstemon	Widely used in California. Annual in cold-winter areas.	🦌 💧
Philodendron spp.	Philodendron	A hardy tropical. Prefers southern coast.	🪟
Phormium spp.	New Zealand flax	Tolerates extremes in heat, not cold.	🦌 🪟 💧
Senecio cineraria	Dusty miller	Grows anywhere below 5,000 feet.	🦌 💧
Stachys byzantina	Lamb's ears	The shorter the winter, the better it grows.	🦌
Strelitzia spp.	Bird of paradise	A tropical that dislikes cold. Thrives along southern coast.	🦌 💧
Zantedeschia spp.	Calla	Grows everywhere but in desert and high elevations. Will naturalize in wet winter climates.	🦌

Lamb's ear *(Stachys byzantina)*

Pittosporum tobira 'Wheeler's Dwarf," Mondo grass ***(Liriope* spp.)**, and rock are effectively used to control erosion on this high-traffic slope.

Ferns for Firescaping

Ferns are some of the oldest plants used for landscaping in California. Like few other plant families, this diverse bunch enjoys longevity and popularity. Little wonder for their success, though: With hundreds of varieties, there is one that will satisfy the most fickle person or environment; they are absolutely deer proof; and, along with being fire retardant, many varieties will resprout after being burned to the ground, sometimes within days after a deep watering. Ferns definitely have a run on favorable characteristics.

While there are ferns that thrive in alpine and desert environments, most do not. The majority of ferns prefer moist and cool conditions. They like filtered shade, and rich and moist soil. They are a bastion for the north and east sides of our houses. Below are the most common varieties of the Polypodiaceae family of ferns (because they posses the majority).

Botanical Name	Common Name	Care and Habitat
Adiantum spp.	Maidenhair fern	Grows everywhere except desert and hot, dry heat.
Asplenium bulbiferum	Mother fern	Prefers moisture and needs protection from freeze.
Athyrium nipponicum 'Pictum'	Japanese painted fern	Grows anywhere that can be protected from hot and dry air.
Blechnum spicant	Deer fern	Native to and prefers the conditions of northern California, even alpine.
Cyrtomium falcatum	Holly fern	Needs protection from frost and prefers moist conditions.
Davallia trichomanoides	Squirrel's foot fern	Grows outside along southern coast, inside elsewhere.
Dryopteris arguta	California wood fern	Its range stretches the wooded portions of the state.
Mattauccia struthiopteris	Ostrich fern	From alpine to southern coast, nothing stops it but hot, dry climates.
Microlepia strigosa	Lace fern	While water-conserving, it needs protection from extremes in temperature.
Nephrolepis cordifolia	Southern sword fern	Needs protection from heat and freeze, but can become a nuisance along the coast.
Polypodium glycyrrhiza	Licorice fern	Native to and prefers California's coast.
Polystichum munitum	Sword fern	A native to California's wooded, coastal environments.
Rumohra adiantiformis, sometimes sold as *Aspidium capense*	Leather leaf fern	Needs protection from extremes in heat and cold.

CHAPTER 7

CHAPTER 7

Shrubs

Botanical Name	Common Name	Care and Habitat	Characteristics
Brunfelsia pauciflora	Yesterday-today-and-tomorrow	Prefers coast, requires shade inland.	
Camellia spp.	Camellia	Likes humidity and dislikes extremes. *C. sasanqua* can tolerate more heat and sun.	[deer] [fire]
Coprosma spp.	Coprosma	Tough in mild winters.	[deer] [anchor] [fire] [water]
Escallonia spp.	Escallonia	Prefers coastal influence. Dislikes extremes. *E. illinita* has resinous fragrance and should be avoided.	[fire] [water]
Gardenia jasminoides	Gardenia	Prefers drier seasons, no frost.	
Hibiscus rosa-sinensis	Tropical hibiscus	Prefers coastal humidity.	[fire]
Ligustrum spp.	Privet	With water, it can grow in anything but snow.	[fire]
Philadelphus spp.	Mock orange	Only *P. mexicanus* likes southern coast. Other species prefer a freeze.	[fire]
Photinia x fraseri	Photinia	Grows everywhere but areas with hard freezes, snow.	[fire] [water]
Pittosporum crassifolium, P. tobira	Pittosporum	Prefers areas with coastal influence. Fussy in extremes.	[anchor] [fire] [water]
Rhaphiolepis spp.	Rhaphiolepis	Can tolerate mild freezes, likes sun. Hard to grow in high desert and in long, wet winters.	[fire] [water]
Rhododendron spp.	Rhododendron, azalea	Fantastic range, grows throughout California. Azalea hybrids aren't deer resistant.	[deer] [fire]
Rosa spp.	Rose	Grows throughout California. Some varieties are good for erosion control.	
Syringa spp.	Lilac	Performs best in areas with a pronounced winter. Risky along central and southern coasts.	[deer] [fire]
Syzygium paniculatum	Brush cherry	Grows in any frost-free landscape. Forms as small tree if not pruned.	[fire]
Thevetia peruviana	Yellow oleander	Will thrive in any amount of heat and sun, but a frost will hurt it.	[deer] [fire] [water]
Vaccinium ovatum	Evergreen huckleberry	Native to northern and central coasts. Likes a mild climate, dislikes extremes.	
Viburnum macrocephalum, V. plicatum	Chinese snowball, Japanese snowball	Grows everywhere but in desert.	[fire]
Xylosma congestum	Xylosma	Grows everywhere but at high elevations.	[anchor] [fire] [water]

Trees			
Botanical Name	**Common Name**	**Care and Habit**	**Characteristics**
Acer spp.	Maple	Prefers northern and central coasts and desert. All but *A. palmatum* is stunted in southern California. Sometimes deer resistant.	(leaf) (water drop)
Betula spp.	Birch	Somewhat tolerant of freeze, not of desert heat.	(leaf)
Cercis spp.	Redbud	Grows everywhere but at highest elevations.	(leaf) (deer)
Cornus spp.	Dogwood	Grows throughout California.	(leaf)
Dracaena draco	Dragon tree	Likes sunny and mild central and southern coasts.	
Feijoa sellowiana	Pineapple guava	Tolerates any amount of heat. Dislikes freezes and foggy coastal conditions.	(curtain) (water drop)
Ficus spp.	Ficus	Grows throughout California. All are deer resistant and most need little water once established.	(curtain) (deer)
Fraxinus spp.	Ash	Grows throughout California.	(leaf) (deer) (water drop)
Griselinia spp.	Griselinia	Hard to grow in freezes and deserts.	(curtain)
Lagerstroemia indica	Crape myrtle	Needs definite seasons. The hotter the summer, the better. A prolonged freeze will kill it.	(leaf) (deer) (water drop)
Liquidambar spp.	Sweet gum	Likes all but desert heat. The more pronounced the seasons, the better fall color.	(leaf) (deer)
Magnolia spp.	Magnolia	Prefers mild, coastal climates.	(deer) (curtain)
Malus spp.	Crabapple	Can tolerate a lot of heat. Needs a chilly winter to flower.	(leaf)
Maytenus boaria	Mayten	Needs distinct seasons, but dislikes the extremes of either.	(deer) (curtain)
Michelia spp.	Michelia	Prefers southern coast. Does well in fog.	
Pittosporum eugenioides, P. rhombifolium, P. undulatum	Pittosporum	Prefers coastal climate. Fussy in extremes.	(curtain) (water drop)
Podocarpus spp.	Podocarpus	Prefers coastal climate.	(deer) (curtain)
Pyrus spp.	Ornamental pear	Deciduous varieties grow everywhere but in desert. Evergreen varieties dislike a freeze, prefers coast.	(leaf) (water drop)

CHAPTER 7

Trees, cont.			
Botanical Name	**Common Name**	**Care and Habitat**	**Characteristics**
Schefflera pueckleri (also known as *Tupi-danthus calyptratus*)	Tupidanthus	A tropical that likes sunny central and southern coasts.	
Schinus molle	California pepper	Versatile, but dislikes extremes of deserts and mountains.	
Strelitzia nicolai	Giant bird of paradise	Grows along coast and in low deserts. Cannot tolerate frost.	

Giant bird of paradise *(Strelitza nicolai)* and Lily-of-the-Nile provide a formidable defense against the fire that will eventually clear the landscape across the street.

California pepper *(Schinus molle)*

A Fruity Defense

Some are deciduous and dramatic, others are evergreen and fragrant, but all are excellent for fire protection. Fruit trees have many traits that make them ideal plants for zone 1. They have supple and moist leaves, do not produce a great amount of fuel, many resprout if injured in a fire, and they all produce a wonderful treat.

More likely than not, fruit trees like full sun, dislike extremes in soil moisture, and, if nothing else, they require biannual pruning. Picking the right tree for the right environment saves maintenance time and heartache.

Apple:	There are enough varieties to ensure that almost anyone in California can grow one.
Apricot:	Grows anywhere but the soupy southern California coast.
Cherry:	Likes a pronounced winter, but a mild summer.
Citrus:	Can be grown anywhere temperatures stay above 20°F. Includes grapefruit, kumquat, lemon, lime, orange, tangelo, and tangerine.
Peach/Nectarines:	From the deserts to the mountaintops, there's a variety for almost every corner of California.
Pear:	Likes a pronounced winter, but a mild summer.
Persimmon:	Good for most of southern California, in foothills, and warm valleys.
Plum/Prune:	Grows anywhere but in high elevations and the soupy southern coast.

Vines			
Botanical Name	**Common Name**	**Care and Habitat**	**Characteristics**
Campsis spp.	Trumpet vine, trumpet creeper	Hardy. Needs a chill for best blooms. Aggressive.	🍁 🦌 💧
Clematis spp.	Clematis	Best performance and selection along the northern coast.	🍁 🦌 💧
Distictis spp.	Trumpet vine	Will tolerate lows to 24°F, but does better along coast.	
Ficus pumila	Creeping fig	Lows below 28°F will cause dieback. Can tolerate any amount of heat. Durable.	🦌 💧
Hibbertia scandens	Guinea gold vine	Best along southern coast. Dislikes even a light frost. Grows along entire coast with some success.	🦌 💧
Jasminum spp.	Jasmine	Grows everywhere but in extreme temperatures. *J. nudiflorum* and *J. officinale* are deciduous.	🦌
Pandorea jasminoides	Bower vine	Prefers the southern coast. No wind.	🦌
Parthenocissus tricuspidata	Boston ivy	Evergreen in mild winters. Likes shade in desert.	🍁
Podranea ricasoliana	Pink trumpet vine	Thrives in heat, but will drop leaves in frost.	💧
Rosa polyanthas	Shrub rose	Grows throughout California.	🍁
Trachelospermum jasminoides	Star jasmine	Grows in most places throughout California, but prolonged freezes will cause death.	
Vitis spp.	Grape	Grows well in both heat and freeze. Seek local references for best variety.	🍁
Wisteria spp.	Wisteria	Grows throughout California. Regular pruning will help flower production and appearance.	🍁 🦌 💧

Wisteria

Zone 2: Greenbelt/Fuel Break

Extending 31 to 70 feet from a structure, and much farther on slopes, this zone will stop a ground fire. Plants recommended in zone 2 are considered the most fire retardant because they maintain low fuels and high moisture despite droughts, freezes, infestations, and possible neglect. Trees and shrubs are kept isolated and only used to serve a variety of functions, such as privacy, heat and cold reduction, and wildlife enhancement. Ground covers grow no higher than 18 inches. Picking plants that are compatible with the naturally occurring conditions is critical to the success of this zone.

CHAPTER 7

Ground Covers
Succulents

As a general rule, succulents dislike a freeze and most do not thrive in the desert's summer heat. Most succulents prefer California's coast. Only a few of these plants will survive after fire. When succulents can be successfully grown, there is no better plant for retarding a fire.

Succulents			
Botanical Name	**Common Name**	**Care and Habitat**	**Characteristics**
Aeonium simsii	Aeonium	Prefers sunny coastal climate. Dislikes extremes.	💧
Aloe aristata, A. ciliaris, A. distans, A. saponaria	Aloe	Tolerates any amount of heat, but is sensitive to frost. Easy to grow in right conditions.	🦌 💧
Carpobrotus spp.	Ice plant	Will die back in freezes. *C. chilensis* is native to coast, good in sand.	💧
Crassula corymbulosa, C. lactea, C. lycopodioides, C. multicava, C. schmidtii	Crassula	Grows along entire coast. Needs protection from frost.	💧
Delosperma spp.	Trailing ice plant	Grows anywhere with mild winters.	💧
Drosanthemum spp.	Trailing ice plant	Prefers coastal climates. *D. floribundum,* is the best for erosion control.	🦌 ⚓ 💧
Echeveria elegans, E. x imbricata, E. secunda	Hens and chicks	Grows only in mild and sunny situations, and on the coast.	
Lampranthus spp.	Ice plant	More versatile than most succulents, but still dislikes the extremes of cold and heat.	💧
Malephora spp.	Ice plant	Dislikes a pronounced winter. Tolerates desert heat.	💧
Sedum acre, S. album, S. anglicum, S. confusum, S. lineare, S. spathulifolium	Stonecrop	Although species vary in hardiness, they are typically tougher than most succulents.	💧
Senecio mandraliscae, S. serpens	Senecio	Needs protection from frost. Tolerates any amount of heat.	

Where they can be grown, cacti and succulents provide dramatic forms, creating unique landscapes.

Senecio mandraliscae and a variety of sedums are providing protection in the midst of sage scrub.

Non-Succulent Ground Covers

Botanical Name	Common Name	Care and Habitat	Characteristics
Achillea ageratifolia, A. clavennae, A. tomentosa	Greek yarrow, silvery yarrow, woolly yarrow	Grows throughout California with little difficulty. *A. clavennae* is lower growing.	[deer] [drought]
Ambrosia chamissonis	Silver beachweed	Prefers northern and southern coasts. Needs temperatures to remain above 30°F.	[drought]
Arabis spp.	Rockcress	*A. blepharophylla* is native to northern coast. All others need a pronounced winter.	[drought]
Arctotheca calendula	Cape weed	Can tolerate a light freeze. Prefers coast.	[deer] [drought] [anchor]
Artemisia caucasica	Silver spreader	Grows throughout California. Tolerates extremes.	[deer] [anchor] [drought]
Atriplex semibaccata	Australian saltbush	Dislikes extremes. Hardy plant for tough conditions in mild climates.	[deer] [anchor] [drought]
Aurinia saxatilis	Basket-of-gold	Grows everywhere but in extreme winters.	
Cerastium tomentosum	Snow-in-summer	Grows throughout California. Sometimes short lived.	[deer] [drought]
Cistus salviifolius	Sageleaf rockrose	Thrives along northern and southern coasts. Tolerates hot summers. Dies back at 15°F.	[deer] [anchor] [drought]
Convolvulus mauritanicus	Ground morning glory	Tolerates any amount of heat. Prefers mild-winter areas.	[drought]
Coprosma x kirkii, C. pumila	Coprosma	Very durable in mild winters.	[deer] [anchor] [drought]
Coreopsis auriculata 'Nana'	Tickseed	Tolerates heat. Dislikes a prolonged frost. Best along northern and southern coasts.	[drought]
Cotoneaster dammeri	Bearberry cotoneaster	Hardy everywhere but in snow.	[anchor] [drought]
Duchesnea indica	Indian mock strawberry	Grows throughout California.	
Erigeron spp.	Santa Barbara daisy, seaside daisy, fleabane	Can tolerate a frost, but prefers coast.	[deer] [drought]
Euonymus fortunei	Prostrate mirror plant	Hardy. Prefers summer heat and winter frost.	[deer] [anchor] [drought]
Fragaria chiloensis, F. californica	Wild strawberry, sand strawberry	Native to Pacific Coast. Needs water farther inland.	[deer] [drought]

Non-Succulent Ground Covers, cont.

Botanical Name	Common Name	Care and Habitat	Characteristics
Gazania hybrids	Trailing gazania	Can't tolerate hard freezes or long, wet winters. Grows everywhere else, deserts included.	(deer) (water drop)
Myoporum parvifolium	Prostrate myoporum	Likes coast and heat. Dislikes extremes.	(deer) (anchor) (water drop)
Oenothera spp.	Evening primrose	Grows throughout California.	(deer) (water drop)
Osteospermum fruticosum	African daisy, freeway daisy	Tolerates heat. Prolonged freeze can cause death. Sometimes short lived, 3–6 years.	(deer) (water drop)
Phyla nodiflora	Lippia	Tolerates heat, but not a lot of cold.	(deer)
Teucrium chamaedrys, T. cossonii majoricum	Germander	Grows throughout California.	(deer) (water drop)
Trifolium fragiferum	Strawberry clover	Grows everywhere but in areas with hard freezes. If watered, it is a good lawn substitute.	(deer) (anchor) (water drop)
Trifolium repens	White clover	Grows throughout California. Able to fixate nitrogen.	
Verbena peruviana, V. pulchella gracilior, V. tenuisecta	Verbena, moss verbena	Grows everywhere but at highest elevations. Prefers dry heat. V. peruviana is deer resistant.	(water drop)

Perennials

Botanical Name	Common Name	Care and Habitat	Characteristics
Achillea filipendulina, A. millefolium, A. ptarmica	Yarrow	Grows throughout California.	(deer) (water drop)
Artemisia ludoviciana albula	Silver king	Grows throughout California.	(deer) (water drop)
Artemisia stellerana	Dusty miller	Better in cold winters than other so-called dusty millers.	(deer) (water drop)
Chrysanthemum hosmariense	Coastal chrysanthemum	As the name suggests, it prefers a coastal garden.	
Coreopsis maritima	Coastal coreopsis	Native to southern coast. Will naturalize.	(deer) (water drop)
Dietes bicolor, D. vegeta	African iris, fortnight lily, moraea	Thrives along entire coast and Central Valley. Dislikes extremes.	(deer) (water drop)
Eschscholzia californica	California poppy	Grows throughout California.	(deer) (anchor) (water drop)
Euphorbia characias, E. myrsinites, E. rigida	Euphorbia	Tolerate most environments, except snowy elevations.	(deer) (water drop)

CHAPTER 7

Perennials, cont.

Botanical Name	Common Name	Care and Habitat	Characteristics
Gaura lindheimeri	Gaura	Grows throughout California. Prefers pronounced summers.	💧
Heuchera maxima	Island alum root	Native to Channel Islands. Likes heat, but not frost.	💧
Iberis sempervirens	Evergreen candytuft	Good performer in coastal environments.	
Kniphofia uvaria	Red-hot poker	Tolerate most extremes, but not desert heat.	🦌 💧
Limonium latifolium, L. perezii	Sea lavender, statice	Tolerates any amount of heat and hardy to 23°F.	💧
Lotus berthelotii	Parrot's beak	Prefers climates by ocean and thermal belts. Dies back in cold weather.	
Lupinus spp.	Lupine	Native to moister coastal regions and some readily reseed in those areas.	🦌 💧
Lychnis coronaria	Crown-pink, dusty miller	Grows throughout California.	🦌 💧
Oenothera hookeri	Hooker's evening primrose	Native. A hard frost will kill it.	🦌 💧
Plecostachys serpyllifolia	Silver mound	Prefers mild climate. Dislikes desert and high elevations.	🦌 💧
Salvia argentea	Silver sage	Grows throughout California. Likes sun.	🦌 💧
Verbena bonariensis	Standing verbena	Grows without snow and excessive winter moisture.	💧
Xanthorrhoea spp.	Grass tree	Grows well along coast and in mild climates.	🦌 💧

Silver king *(Artemisia ludoviciana albula)*

Red-hot poker *(Kniphofia uvaria)* and standing verbena *(Verbena bonariensis)*

CHAPTER 7

Shrubs: Succulents and Cacti

Botanical Name	Common Name	Care and Habitat	Characteristics
Aeonium spp.	Aeonium	Prefers ocean influence. Dislikes extremes.	💧
Agave spp.	Agave	Tolerances vary with species. Most, however, will die back in a freeze. Prefers sunny coast.	🦌 💧
Aloe arborescens, A. bainesii, A. striata, A. variegata, A. vera	Aloe	Best suited for central and southern California.	💧
Carnegiea gigantea	Saguaro	Tolerates any amount of heat. Tolerates only a mild freeze. Does not grow directly on coast.	🦌 💧
Cotyledon spp.	Cotyledon	Thrives along sunny coast. Dislikes extreme heat.	💧
Crassula arborescens, C. argentea, C. falcata	Crassula	Likes sunny coast. Needs protection from frost.	💧
Doryanthes palmeri	Spear lily	Prefers sunny coast. Dislikes extremes.	
Dudleya spp.	Cliff lettuce	Native to coastal cliffs and hills. Likes sunny, mild climates.	💧
Echeveria gibbiflora, E. hybrids	Echeveria	Likes sun, but not extremes.	💧
Echinocactus spp.	Barrel cactus	Tolerates lows to 20ºF and any amount of heat.	🦌 💧
Echinopsis spp.	Easter lily cactus	Needs protection from frost and intense heat.	💧
Ferocactus spp.	Barrel cactus	Adapted to desert, not high elevations or wet coast.	🦌 💧
Haworthia spp.	Haworthia	Tolerates frost, but not freeze.	🦌 💧
Opuntia spp.	Prickly pear, pancake cactus	Likes heat. Will die back during an extended frost.	🦌 🎭 💧
Sedum dendroideum, S. d. praealtum, S. oxypetalum, S. spectabile, S. telephium	Stonecrop	Although species vary in hardiness, they are typically tougher than most succulents.	💧
Stenocereus thurberi	Organpipe cactus	Can survive a frost, but no freeze.	🦌 💧

CHAPTER 7

Shrubs: Non-Succulent

Botanical Name	Common Name	Care and Habitat	Characteristics
Atrilplex spp.	Saltbush	Dislikes extremes. Hardy plant for tough situations in mild climates.	🦌 ⚓ 💧
Cistus purpureus	Orchid rockrose	Thrives in climates influenced by the ocean, in the north and south. Dies back at 15°F.	🦌 ⚓ 💧
Convolvulus cneorum	Bush morning glory	Prefers mild winter and summer heat.	🦌 💧
Dasylirion spp.	Tree grass, desert spoon	A native that prefers dry heat and mild winters.	🦌 💧
Helianthemum nummularium	Sunrose	Grows in all areas without hard freeze.	💧
Lavatera assurgentiflora	Tree mallow	Native to Channel Islands. Likes heat and sun. Dislikes extremes.	💧
Leucophyllum spp.	Texas ranger, silverleaf	Grows in all areas, except those with extreme winters.	🦌 🪟 💧
Myoporum debile, M. 'Pacificum'	Myoporum	Likes a coastal influence and heat. Dislikes extremes.	🦌 ⚓ 🪟 💧
Nerium oleander	Oleander	Likes heat and tolerates mild freezes. Dislikes shade and dampness.	🦌 🪟 💧
Nolina spp.	Mexican grass tree	Native to desert.	🦌 💧
Punica granatum 'Chico,' 'Nana'	Dwarf pomegranate	Does well in long summers. Tolerates a mild freeze. Tough.	🦌 💧
Rhus integrifolia	Lemonade berry	Native to southern coast. Prefers the coast. Dislikes extremes.	🦌 ⚓ 🪟 💧
Rhus ovata	Sugar bush	Native to dry southern foothills. Tolerates extremes better than other *Rhus* species.	🦌 🪟 💧
Simmondsia chinensis	Jojoba	Native to southern deserts. Takes any amount of heat. Dislikes freezes.	🦌 🪟 💧
Yucca whipplei	Our Lord's candle	Native to southern coast and hills. Tolerates a wide range of climates, except high elevations.	🦌 💧

CHAPTER 7

Tree mallow (*Lavatera assurgentiflora*)

A hedge of oleander (*Nerium oleander*) is broken up with interest by bird of paradise (*Strelitzia reginae*).

Trees			
Botanical Name	**Common Name**	**Care and Habitat**	**Characteristics**
Arbutus unedo	Strawberry tree	Grows throughout California, except in areas with coldest winters. Hardy.	🦌 🪟 💧
Ceratonia siliqua	Carob	Prefers coastal climates.	🦌 ⚓ 💧
Cercis occidentalis	Western redbud	Native to foothills below 4,000 feet. Tough and tolerates freeze.	🍁 🦌 ⚓ 💧
Cupaniopsis anacardioides	Carrot wood	Likes sunny central and southern coasts.	💧
Fraxinus dipetala	Foothill ash	Native to central and southern foothills. Durable. Likes long summers and can withstand freezes, except in high elevations.	🍁 🦌 💧
Gleditsia triacanthos	Honey locust	Tolerates extremes. Dislikes coastal areas without definite seasons.	🍁 🦌
Macadamia spp.	Macadamia nut	Great along coasts and thermal belts. Dislikes extremes.	💧
Myoporum insulare, M. laetum	Myoporum	Likes a coastal influence and heat. Dislikes extremes.	🦌 ⚓ 🪟 💧
Pistacia chinensis	Chinese pistache	Doesn't tolerate extreme cold. Likes heat.	🦌 🍁 ⚓ 💧
Quercus kelloggii	California black oak	A native found throughout California. Dislikes desert and areas along southern coast.	🍁 🦌 ⚓ 💧
Rhus lancea	African sumac	Likes heat, but not prolonged frosts or freeze.	🦌 🪟 💧
Tamarix spp.	Tamarisk	Tough. Excellent in wind and drought. Competitive roots. *T. chinensis* (salt cedar) is a weed and should be avoided.	🦌 🪟 💧

Trees, cont.			
Botanical Name	**Common Name**	**Care and Habitat**	**Characteristics**
Yucca aloifolia	Spanish bayonet	Grows everywhere but in high elevations.	
Yucca brevifolia	Joshua tree	Prefers short winters and long summers. Dramatic.	
Yucca elata	Soaptree yucca	Prefers short winters and long summers.	
Yucca elephantipes, Y. gloriosa, Y. recurvifolia	Giant yucca, Spanish dagger	Needs protection from extremes, including intense heat.	

Vines			
Botanical Name	**Common Name**	**Care and Habitat**	**Characteristics**
Antigonon leptopus	Coral vine	Needs a pronounced, mild winter. Likes heat.	
Parthenocissus inserta, P. quinquefolia	Virginia creeper	Grows throughout California. *P. quinquefolia* can help control erosion.	
Rosa banksiae	Lady Banks' rose	Grows everywhere but at highest elevations. Very reliable.	
Senecio confusus	Mexican flame vine	Likes a climate strongly influenced by coast. Dislikes frost and freeze.	
Solanum wendlandii	Costa Rican nightshade	Likes heat, not frosts or soupy summers.	
Tecomaria capensis	Cape honeysuckle	Thrives along sunny coast, likes heat. Needs protection from frost.	

Zone 3: Transition Zone

Starting 71 feet from a house to 120 feet, and much farther out on slopes, this zone dramatically slows a fire. The recommended plants are considered fire resistant rather than fire retardant. Fire resistant means that these plants resist the effects of fire and may resprout or germinate after a fire. When selecting plants for the transition zone, look for those that are broadleaf, low maintenance, noninvasive, and have the ability to grow in the naturally occurring conditions.

CHAPTER 7

CHAPTER 7

Ground Covers

Botanical Name	Common Name	Care and Habitat	Characteristics
Abronia spp.	Sand verbena	Native to and prefers coastal conditions in north and south.	🦌 ⚓ 💧
Arctostaphylos densiflora	Vine hill manzanita	Native to Sonoma County. Dislikes extremes.	🦌 ⚓ 💧
Arctostaphylos edmundsii	Little Sur manzanita	Native to Monterey County. Likes sunny coast.	🦌 ⚓ 💧
Arctostaphylos 'Emerald Green'	Emerald green manzantia	Grows along entire coast. Dislikes extremes. Greenest of all manzanitas.	🦌 ⚓ 💧
Arctostaphylos nummularia	Fort Bragg manzanita	Grows along entire coast.	🦌 ⚓ 💧
Arctostaphylos pumila	Dune manzanita	Native to Monterey County. Best manzanitia in soupy conditions.	🦌 ⚓ 💧
Arctostaphylos uva-ursi	Bearberry	Native to San Mateo County. Grows everywhere but in desert.	🦌 ⚓ 💧
Baccharis pilularis 'Twin Peaks'	Dwarf coyote brush	Native to coast, and grows best near it.	🦌 ⚓ 💧
Carissa macrocarpa 'Green Carpet'	Natal plum	Although best along sunny central and southern coasts, it tolerates the desert. Dislikes a prolonged freeze.	🦌 ⚓ 💧
Ceanothus gloriosus	Point Reyes ceanothus	Northern coast native. Dislikes intense heat.	🦌 ⚓ 💧
Ceanothus griseus horizontalis	Carmel creeper	Grows everywhere but in areas with long, cold winters.	⚓ 💧
Ceanothus prostratus, C. p. occidentalis	Squaw carpet ceanothus	*C. prostratus* does better in higher elevations. *C. p. occidentalis* prefers lower, milder climates.	⚓ 💧
Cotoneaster adpressus	Creeping cotoneaster	Grows throughout California.	⚓ 💧
Cotoneaster horizontalis	Rock cotoneaster	Grows everywhere but in desert.	🦌 ⚓ 💧
Cotoneaster microphyllus	Rockspray cotoneaster	Same as *C. horizontalis*, but smaller.	🦌 ⚓ 💧
Gaultheria procumbens	Wintergreen	Tough in woodland from Bay Area and north. Dislikes strong winter.	🦌 ⚓

Ground Covers, cont.

Botanical Name	Common Name	Care and Habitat	Characteristics
Mahonia nervosa	Longleaf mahonia	Native to, and prefers northern coast.	(deer) (anchor) (water drop)
Mahonia repens	Creeping mahonia	Native to interior. Likes distinct seasons. Dislikes mild southern coast.	(deer) (anchor) (water drop)
Maianthemum dilatatum	False lily-of-the-valley	Native to northern California. An understory perennial. Tolerates any amount of cold. Dislikes heat.	(water drop)
Verbena gooddingii	Desert verbena	Prefers heat. Will naturalize in a sunny and watered environment.	(water drop)

Perennials

Botanical Name	Common Name	Care and Habitat	Characteristics
Aquilegia formosa	Western columbine	Tough plant for sunny understory environments throughout California.	(deer)
Asclepias tuberosa	Milkweed, butterfly weed	Hardy throughout California. Attracts the monarch butterfly, which will visit this native yearly.	(water drop)
Aster chilensis	Wild aster	Coastal native. Dislikes extremes.	(water drop)
Centranthus ruber	Jupiter's beard, red valerian	Dislikes extremes. Hardy in difficult soils.	(deer) (water drop)
Coreopsis gigantea	Giant coreopsis	Native to southern coast.	(deer) (water drop)
Encelia spp.	Encelia	Native to sunny coast, prefers the same.	(water drop)
Erysimum spp.	Wallflower	With so many varieties, there is one that will grow in your garden.	(deer)
Gaillardia spp.	Blanket flower	Grows throughout California. Likes hot summers.	(deer) (water drop)
Helichrysum petiolare	Licorice plant	Likes the sunny coast. Dislikes frost.	(deer)
Iris douglasiana, I. innominata, I. tenax	Pacific Coast irises	Grows throughout California. Dependable.	(deer) (water drop)
Paeonia californica	Peony	Although it requires definite seasons, it dislikes their extremes.	
Penstemon centranthifolius	Scarlet bugler	Does best along southern coast.	(deer) (water drop)

CHAPTER 7

Perennials, cont.

Botanical Name	Common Name	Care and Habitat	Characteristics
Perovskia atriplici-folia	Russian sage	Although it can grow anywhere, it prefers pronounced winter.	
Romneya coulteri	Matilija poppy	A southern California native that can be grown throughout California.	
Salvia spathacea	Crimson sage, hummingbird sage	Tolerates a lot of heat, but dies back in a long winter.	
Sisyrinchium bellum, S. californicum	Blue-eyed grass, yellow-eyed grass	Grows throughout California except in snowy elevations. *S. californicum* needs more water.	
Trillium ovatum	Wake robin	An understory native that prefers northern California's moisture.	
Triteleia laxa	Grass nut	Pacific Coast native. Tolerates heat and drought.	
Zauschneria californica	California fuchsia	Useful everywhere but at high elevations.	

Pacific coast irises *(Iris douglasiana)*

Matilija poppy *(Romneya coulteri)*, manzanita, and a variety of well-maintained salvias are part of this effective transition zone.

Shrubs			
Botanical Name	**Common Name**	**Care and Habitat**	**Characteristics**
Calycanthus occidentalis	Spice bush	Native to streams and moist slopes along California's coast. Likes the same.	
Carissa macrocarpa	Natal plum	Although best along sunny central and southern coasts, tolerates desert. Dislikes a prolonged freeze.	
Carpenteria californica	Bush anemone	A native from Sierra Nevada to Fresno County. Can take frost and a mild freeze.	
Ceanothus griseus spp.	Ceanothus	Dislikes long winters and deserts.	
Ceanothus thyrsiflorus	Blue blossom	Hardier than other species, but freezes in long winters.	
Cistus purpureus	Orchid rockrose	Thrives along northern and southern coasts. OK in hot summers, but dies back at 15°F.	
Cistus salviifolius	Sageleaf rockrose	Same as above.	
Correa spp.	Australian fuchsia	Likes dry coastal conditions. Not fussy.	
Cotoneaster apiculatus	Cranberry cotoneaster	Grows throughout California.	
Cotoneaster lacteus	Red clusterberry	Grows in all but coldest winters.	
Dendromecon harfordii	Island bush poppy	Grows anywhere along coast.	
Galvezia speciosa	Island bush snapdragon	Native to southern coast. Prefers mild winters.	
Gaultheria shallon	Salal	Hardy native. Prefers woodland environments. In southern California's sun it is a small shrub.	
Heteromeles arbutifolia	Toyon, Christmas berry	Grows everywhere, but in snow.	
Isomeris arborea	Bladderpod, burro fat	A southern California native found along coastal dunes to low deserts. Dislikes freezes.	
Mahonia aquifolium	Oregon grape	Native to northern California. Needs a pronounced winter.	
Mahonia fremontii	Desert mahonia	Native to deserts. Grows everywhere but in hard freezes, snow.	
Mahonia pinnata	California holly grape	Found and grown throughout California. Dislikes extremes.	

Shrubs, cont.

Botanical Name	Common Name	Care and Habitat	Characteristics
Myrica californica	Pacific wax myrtle	Native to coast and coastal valleys, north and south. Grows 21°F–90°F.	
Prunus ilicifolia	Hollyleaf cherry	Native to northern and southern coastal ranges. Likes heat and dry conditions. A prolonged freeze will kill it.	
Prunus laurocerasus	English laurel	Best along moist, northern coast. OK to 5°F. Dislikes dry deserts.	
Prunus lyonii	Catalina cherry	Native to Channel Islands. Good in dry heat and will tolerate all but hard freezes.	
Rhamnus californica	Coffeeberry	A native found and grown throughout California. Dislikes high elevations.	
Rhamnus crocea ilicifolia	Holleyleaf redberry	A native that prefers distinct and dry seasons. Dislikes moist coastal conditions and high elevations.	
Rhododendron occidentale	Western azalea	A hardy and versatile native. Grows everywhere but at highest elevations.	
Ribes speciosum	Fuchsia-flowering gooseberry	Native to Santa Clara County and southward. Dislikes extremes. Deciduous leaves in intense heat.	
Salvia greggii	Red-lipped sage, autumn sage	Grows throughout California, except in moist conditions and at high elevations.	
Salvia leucantha	Mexican bush sage	Native to southern California. Grows along entire coast. Dislikes high elevations.	
Salvia sonomensis	Creeping sage, Sonoma sage	Prefers sunny, dry climates. Dislikes pronounced winters.	
Senecio greyi	Senecio	Grows throughout California, except in deserts and at high elevations.	
Solanum xantii	Nightshade	A native that grows everywhere but in deserts and at high elevations.	
Teucrium fruticans	Bush germander	Grows throughout California, except in high elevations.	

Island bush poppy (*Dendromecon harfordii*)

This meadowlike planting of native plants provides many benefits, including excellent fire protection and habitat enhancement.

CHAPTER 7

Trees			
Botanical Name	**Common Name**	**Care and Habitat**	**Characteristics**
Acer macrophyllum	Bigleaf maple	Native to and best in northern California. Likes distinct seasons, deserts included. Dislikes mild, warm environments.	[leaf] [deer] [water]
Aesculus californica	California buckeye	Native to slopes and canyons below 4,000 feet. Needs seasons, but dislikes their extremes.	[leaf] [deer] [water]
Alnus rhombifolia	White alder	A native found in the foothills. Tolerates a freeze. Dislikes deserts and southern coast. Tall.	[leaf] [deer] [water]
Arbutus menziesii	Madrone	A native that prefers northern coast and southern interior.	[deer] [anchor] [water]
Cercocarpus spp.	Mountain mahogany	A native grown throughout California. Durable. *C. betuloides* is preferred in milder climates.	[deer] [curtain] [water]
Eucalyptus microtheca	Coolibah	Durable. Tolerates low temperatures well. A clean windbreak.	[deer] [anchor] [water]
Eucalyptus spathulata	Narrow-leafed gimlet	Will tolerate lows in teens and heat.	[deer] [anchor] [curtain] [water]
Metrosideros excelsus	New Zealand Christmas tree	Best in mild northern and southern coastal climates.	[deer] [water]
Populus spp.	Aspen, cottonwood, poplar	Requirements vary. *P. fremontii* is native to central and southern coastal valleys. Some have aggressive roots.	[leaf]
Quercus agrifolia	Coast live oak	Native to coastal ranges. Dislikes high elevations.	[deer] [anchor] [curtain] [water]
Quercus douglasii	Blue oak	A Central Valley native that can grow throughout California. Prefers dry heat.	[leaf] [deer] [anchor] [water]
Quercus lobata	Valley oak	A native to dry slopes. Grows everywhere but directly along the northern and southern coasts.	[leaf] [deer] [anchor] [water]
Salix lasiolepis	Arroyo willow	A native to streams. Prefers distinct seasons, but dislikes their extremes.	[leaf]
Sambucus caerulea	Blue elderberry	A native to northern California. Prefers distinct seasons. There are subspecies that perform better in deserts, sunny central and southern California.	[leaf]

Vines			
Botanical Name	**Common Name**	**Care and Habitat**	**Characteristics**
Gelsemium sempervirens	Carolina jessamine	Grows everywhere but in heavy freeze. Somewhat tolerant of low water.	🦌 ⚓
Macfadyena unguis-cati	Yellow trumpet vine	Likes long summers. Dislikes heavy freeze. Tough, aggressive. Semi-deciduous.	💧
Plumbago auriculata	Cape plumbago	Best along a sunny coast. Dislikes extremes. In mild deserts it is a shrub. Erosion controlling along coast.	🦌 💧
Solanum jasminoides	Potato vine	Evergreen in mild climates. Dislikes extremes. Sometimes deciduous.	🦌 💧

Flammable Plants

The plants listed in this section should be avoided—they should neither be planted nor encouraged around a structure. Most of the plants listed below are easily ignitable and highly combustible. Many of these plants ignite without direct flame contact. However, sometimes it does not make economic or ecological sense to remove some of these plants. Instead, follow the care instructions described in this section to minimize fire danger.

Coyote brush, *Baccharis pilularis*, is a good example. In autumn, this flammable shrub is one of the few nectar plants in the coastal scrub communities. There are hundreds of insects that interact with this shrub. One of them, the tachinid fly, is the largest fly in California and although it looks menacing, it is known to eat caterpillars from nearby crops. If this shrub is within 100 feet of a structure, it will need to be maintained to reduce the risk it poses.

Three traits will put a plant on this list: If it is highly ignitable, produces a lot of fuel, and/or it is invasive. All three traits can be minimized by maintenance. Watering in summer can increase moisture levels and reduce ignitability. Regular raking and pruning will reduce fuels.

Invasive species can be controlled by weed-whacking, pulling, or tilling.

The coast redwood, *Sequoia sempervirens*, is considered fire prone because of the enormous amount of litter it produces in late summer and early autumn. Yet if the area and tree is kept clean and slightly moist, the redwood is an excellent garden tree and fire resistant when mature.

The charts that follow list the characteristics that make these plants flammable. If the plant cannot be removed, reduce fire risk by maintaining it. The list also highlights which plants are California natives, which should be researched before removing because of their many possible benefits.

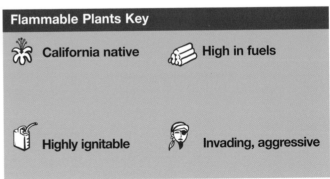

Flammable Plants Key

🌺 California native   🪵 High in fuels

📦 Highly ignitable   🧕 Invading, aggressive

Ground Covers		
Botanical Name	**Common Name**	**Traits**
Auena fatua	Wild oat	
Bromus rubens	Foxtail, red brome	
Hedera canariensis	Algerian ivy	
Hordeum leporinum	Hare, foxtail, annual barley	
Juniperus spp.	Juniper	
Lolium multiflorum	Italian ryegrass, annual ryegrass	
Lonicera japonica	Japanese honeysuckle, Hall's honeysuckle	

Perennials		
Botanical Name	**Common Name**	**Traits**
Agropyron repens	Quackgrass	
Brassica campestris, B. nigra	Field mustard, black mustard	
Cortaderia selloana, C. jubata	Jubata grass, pampas grass,	
Cuscuta pentagona	Dodders, angel's hair	
Foeniculum vulgare	Common fennel	
Miscanthus sinensis	Eulalia, Japanese silver grass	
Muhlenbergia rigens	Deer grass	
Pennisetum setaceum	Fountain grass	

Mustard *(Brassica campestris)* provides a dangerous transition from the sage scrub to a domestic landscape.

Pampas grass *(Cortaderia selloana)* and its large amount of ignitable fuels have overrun this planted bed.

CHAPTER 7

CHAPTER 7

Shrubs

Botanical Name	Common Name	Traits
Adenostoma fasciculatum	Chamis, greasewood	
Adenostoma sparsifolium	Red shanks	
Artemesia abrotanum	Southernwood	
Artemesia absinthium	Wormwood	
Artemisia californica	California sagebrush	
Artemesia dracunculus	True tarragon, French tarragon	
Artemesia tridentata	Big sagebrush	
Baccharis glutinosa	Mule fat	
Baccharis pilularis	Coyote brush	
Castanopsis chrysophylla	Giant chinquapin	
Cytisus canariensis	Canary Island broom	
Cytisus monspessulanus	French broom	
Cytisus scoparius	Scotch broom	
Dodonaea viscosa	Hopseed bush	
Eriodictyon spp.	Yerba santa	
Eriogonum spp.	Buckwheat	
Juniperus spp.	Juniper	
Larix spp.	Larch	

Shrubs, cont.

Botanical Name	Common Name	Traits
Larrea tridentata	Creosote bush	
Leptospermum spp.	Tea tree	
Mimulus aurantiacus longiflorus	Sticky monkey-flower	
Phoradendrom spp., (also Arceuthobium spp.)	Mistletoe (a parasite that can photosynthesize half its usable energy)	
Pickeringia montana	Chaparral pea	
Platycladus orientalis	Oriental arborvitae	
Quercus dumosa	Coastal scrub oak	
Rosmarinus officinalis	Rosemary	
Rubus spp.	Bramble	
Salvia apiana	White sage	
Salvia clevelandii	Cleveland sage	
Salvia leucophylla	Purple sage	
Salvia mellifera	Black sage	
Salvia vaseyi	Wand sage	
Spartium junceum	Spanish broom	
Tamarix chinensis	Salt cedar	
Ulex europaeus	Gorse, forze	

Trees

Botanical Name	Common Name	Traits
Abies spp.	Fir	(flower, logs, milk carton)
Acacia spp.	Acacia, wattle	(logs, milk carton, pirate)
Calocedrus decurrens	Incense cedar	(flower, logs, milk carton)
Casuarina spp.	Beefwood	(milk carton)
Cedrus spp.	Cedar	(logs, milk carton)
Chamaecyparis spp.	False cypress	(flower, logs, milk carton)
Cryptomeria japonica	Japanese cryptomeria	(milk carton)
Cupressocyparis leylandii	Cypress	(logs, milk carton)
Cupressus spp.	Cypress	(flower, logs, milk carton)
Eucalyptus camaldulensis	Red gum eucalyptus	(logs, pirate)
Eucalyptus cladocalyx	Sugar gum eucalyptus	(logs, milk carton, pirate)
Eucalyptus globulus	Blue gum eucalyptus	(logs, milk carton, pirate)
Eucalyptus viminalis	Manna gum eucalyptus	(logs, milk carton, pirate)
Larix spp.	Larch	(logs, milk carton)

Trees, cont.

Botanical Name	Common Name	Traits
Lithocarpus densiflorus	Tanbark oak	(flower, logs, milk carton)
Melaleuca linariifolia	Flaxleaf paperbark	(logs, milk carton)
Palms	Palms (if dead fronds not removed and trunk cleaned)	(milk carton)
Picea spp.	Spruce	(flower, logs, milk carton)
Pinus spp.	Pine	(flower, logs, milk carton, pirate)
Pseudotsuga macrocarpa	Bigcone spruce	(flower, logs, milk carton)
Pseudotsuga menziesii	Douglas fir	(flower, logs, milk carton)
Sequoia sempervirens	Coast redwood	(flower, logs)
Taxodium spp.	Cypress	(logs, milk carton)
Taxus spp.	Yew	(flower, milk carton)
Thuja spp.	Arborvitae	(flower, logs, milk carton)
Tsuga spp.	Hemlock	(flower, logs, milk carton)
Umbellularia californica	California bay	(flower, milk carton, pirate)

The Role of Water in a Firescaped Garden

Water is a valuable resource in any California garden. Tranquil settings and colorful collages are created in a garden through water use. In a firescaped garden, water not only helps create a healthy, fire-retardant landscape, it also helps to put out a fire. Water is a natural source of beauty and safety.

This chapter covers the two roles of water in a firescaped garden: maintenance and emergency systems. Maintenance water is considered the proactive and preventative use of water. Emergency systems are a reactive use of water and are covered last in this chapter. As a sole means of defense, water is unlikely to save a structure in a wildfire. The amount of maintenance hours spent in a garden is the dominant determinant of fire safety. No amount of water can compensate for lack of maintenance.

Maintenance Water

Water conservation is well understood and practiced with frequency in California. However, a plant and landscape's ignitability is directly related to the amount of moisture stored within. As the moisture in a plant's tissues rise, the plant's relative ignitability drops, requiring a hotter fire to ignite it. Unfortunately, fire-retardant, high-water-use landscapes, such as pools, lawns, and tropical plants, are not advised in our water-tight communities.

Adding further friction to the role of water in a firescaped garden are the hundreds of recommended drought-tolerant plants, many of which have flammable characteristics. Plants with small, brittle, waxy, and hairy leaves, and those with high levels of resins and oils, are both water conserving and fire prone.

Simply importing more water to a landscape will not always lower the risk of fire. Improper watering techniques can increase fuels and create water-dependent plants, making an otherwise low-ignition landscape highly ignitable when water is removed. In fact, withholding water from a well-maintained landscape can dramatically lower the plant fuels and maintenance costs, because plants grow to the limit of water's availability.

To balance the roles of water in a garden, firescaping tries to maximize water's potential while minimizing its use. The goal for maintenance water is to retain the highest possible moisture content in plants, while staying within a landscape's water and maintenance budget. There can be a satisfactory compromise between water conservation and fire prevention.

How to Water

How should you water? To a farmer, the answer is easy: Charts and formulas provide guidelines for most crops. Ask every gardener, and you'll receive a different answer. There are no easy formulas, and no two landscapes are alike. However, there are really only two ways to water: using an automatically timed irrigation system or a manually operated irrigation system. Both have advantages and disadvantages.

An automatic watering system is perfect for zone 1 plantings. These plants are broadleaved, supple, and fleshy. They not only need more water but tolerate overwatering, unlike the other, outlying plants. Timers are fairly reliable and can be counted upon when the owners are away. Overwatering, runoff, and complacency are big disadvantages. It's easy to slip into complacency with timers because it appears that if nothing is wilting or dying, everything must be all right. Automatic systems are rarely as efficient as they can be.

A manually operated irrigation system is the most efficient way to water; it gets the water right where it is needed for the length of time needed. The big disadvantage of manual operation is that it requires an attentive person to operate it. Personally turning on the water and checking its progress is especially beneficial on slopes and zone 3 plantings, where deep and infrequent watering is the preferred method.

No matter the method, there is a general framework for watering that ties both together. With California's fire and flood cycles, water must be managed carefully.

Priorities

At the height of the fire season, when plants need water most, water supplies are at their lowest. Water departments are aggressively pushing conservation programs, water rationing may be in effect, and wells are at their lowest levels. Large landscapes become parched during the most dangerous months, September and October. Naturally, water priorities are important to a firescaped garden.

Perspectives: Ken Montgomery, ecologist, horticulturalist, and owner of Anderson Valley Nursery, Boonville

Rockroses are one of my main passions—I grow over 40 kinds. Starting from late May to late June and until the fall rains come, we'll irrigate about once every three weeks, about the equivalent of 1 inch . . . and it is amazing how much higher the moisture content stays in the green tissues, just with that occasional watering. It really helps to maintain a good appearance, too, a little bit more gardenlike, a little less wildlike. And you don't force a lot of summer growth, which is death for most Mediterraneans and natives; to do a lot of growing in the summertime, when they're not supposed to, shortens their life spans. Plants that normally have 30 or more years, well, you can reduce their life span to about 8 to 10 years with too much summer watering.

Although all firescaping zones could use supplemental water, their health should not hinge on this imported resource. Only zone 1, the domestic landscape, can be dependent upon water. Zone 2, the fuel break, has the second highest use of water, but its ability to slow a fire should not depend on imported water. Rather, its ability to slow a fire should be because it is low in fuels.

Water distribution should be prioritized. First, water is used immediately around a structure, then downhill from the structure, and lastly, in the transition areas separating a garden from the natural or native landscapes. If, for any reason, water is taken out of an area that has had it on a semi-regular basis for more than a year, prune and remove plants. The goals are to remove the growth that would eventually become highly ignitable while lowering the need for water in that area.

Water Calendar

California has definite water cycles. Working within these cycles makes the most of available water. Following are the three simplified water cycles found in California: landscapes below 2,000-foot elevation, the northern coast, and higher elevations.

Summer is the dormant season for the landscapes below 2,000 feet. Coastal scrub, chaparral, and oak woodland are a few of the drought-adapted communities. The plants within these communities shed older, less productive growth and eventually slide into a state of dormancy as water availability declines. Summer is their period of rest.

The northern coast differs because of the enormous amount of moisture it receives. Between the rain, which can be as much as 60 inches per year, and the fog, which can contribute as much as 10 inches of precipitation per year, the landscapes are highly productive. However, these landscapes can dry out; Mendocino and Eureka have long histories of fire.

Frozen winters and dry summers make the vegetation in the higher elevations some of the hardiest in the state. Unlike at lower elevations, soil moisture levels can remain high months after the last rain or freeze. However, the demand for this water is great and the conifer forests rapidly pull it up, making these landscapes more prone to fire than the plant communities in the northern coast. Lassen and Tahoe counties and the Santa Cruz Mountains possess this water cycle.

End of Winter to Spring

When the risk of fire is low and a landscape's growth is at its greatest, water is used sparingly and only to sustain a plant's growth. Watering before the soil is completely dry will not only prolong a plant's growth spurt and increase the amount of plant fuels, it will deter the exchange of gases in the soil, which is vital to plant health. Watering can typically wait many weeks after the last rain or freeze. Automatic irrigation systems should be turned on when the first 2 inches of the soil are dry.

Summer to Early Autumn

As the risk of fire increases, deep and infrequent watering will keep a landscape's trees and shrubs less ignitable. Water at this time of year is used to sustain a plant's current level of growth, and not to encourage new growth. Adaptive, native plants should not be watered but instead be encouraged to go dormant by lack of water.

Autumn to First Heavy Rain

The risk of fire has steadily been climbing and it is now at a point of climax; native and natural landscapes can be tinderbox dry. Zone 1 plants should be kept moist. Zones 2 and 3 plants should get water at least twice a month. While the water will wake the adaptive plants prematurely, the risk of fire demands high moisture content in leaves. However, all watering past mid-October should be shallow and aimed only at sustaining health. Ideally, the ground should be dry before autumn's first rain.

Winter

The garden should be taken off all supplemental water and the irrigation system's timer should be turned off. A landscape's water needs are at its lowest. Overwatering is common this time of year. Turn on the water only when the top 2 inches of a soil are completely dry.

Time of Day to Water

Along California's coast, watering should be done in the early morning; mildew and rot are less of a problem if a landscape has a chance to dry. In the drier foothills and mountains, watering should be done during mid-evening, which helps to minimize water evaporation loss.

Timers and Large Irrigation Systems

Automatic watering systems are like politicians: Their goal is not to make everyone happy, but to make the fewest amounts unhappy. Unless the water system is complex and regularly maintained, not all of the plants are going to get the optimum amount of water, which means not every plant will be happy.

However, getting the most out of water is difficult, which is unfortunate because efficiency is not only good for the budget, it improves plant health. Too much water, and oxygen is squeezed out, changing the soil's chemistry. Too little, and dieback occurs. Finding the fulcrum takes work.

More likely than not, a local water district will have a calculator on its website (or a link to one) that will help you determine the amount of water to use, and the amount of time needed to distribute that water. These calculators are attached to a series of questions, up to 12 in some cases. To help ascertain the rate of water, these calculators will ask about soil type, planting type, dominant plants, density of planting, exposure, relative heat, amount of area, slope, and, if applicable, type and rates of flow of existing irrigation systems. If large enough, the water district will also have a director whose primary function is to help homeowners save water. Many large irrigation manufacturers, such as Rain Bird, have fantastic detailed manuals for designing, installing, and maintaining irrigation systems (these are not the superficial pamphlets passed out at high-volume garden retailers).

Canary Plants

No need to buy a water meter—plant one.

A "canary plant" shows the signs of stress before other plants. A canary is sensitive to lack of water and will wilt long before others. It is common to use canaries for the first watering in spring and then again in fall, while trying to dry the soil before the rains. Relative to their rooting depth, these plants can be used as canaries to indicate when a soil is dry: viola, gazania, calla, rose, canna, mallow, grape, lilac, plum, and carrotwood.

Experts agree that there are several general rules about operating large, automatic systems:

Always design and maintain an irrigation line around the most dominant plant type. For instance, if one sprinkler line is watering five shrubs, two trees, and some ground cover, the rate of water is calculated based on the shrubs.

Irrigate compatible plants. Lawn grasses, for example, should never be watered by the same line as the surrounding shrubs; their needs are vastly different.

At a minimum, adjust the time at least four times a year. The timer should be turned off in early winter, timidly back on in late spring, adjusted to greater amounts in midsummer, and turned down in early fall, in preparation for the rain.

Make the timer accessible. Adjusting controls leads to a more efficient system. This will occur only if the control panel is easy, perhaps even pleasurable, to work around.

Keep the system clean. Clogs, common especially in low-flow systems, lead to misdirected water, lack of water, and an increase of water and pressure to other heads, all of which cause changes in the system's distribution patterns. Maintenance should include cleaning and regularly checking filters. Annually flushing out the system will also improve and prolong performance.

If the irrigation system is small and each valve only waters one or two plants, then the information that follows will help determine the amount of time and water needed for plant health.

Manual Irrigation Systems

Deep and infrequent watering is ideal for low-maintenance, drought-tolerant, and zone 3 gardens. The goal behind this method is to train a plant's roots to grow deep, creating a stronger, healthier, and more independent plant. This method does not encourage rapid growth. Also, infrequent watering is conducive to a soil's natural cycle. A soil will never dry at the same rate every week. If a garden were to receive water only when the top 2 inches of soil are dry, the watering would always be infrequent.

Using the deep and infrequent method is simple. First, determine how deep the water should go. Second, determine the amount of time it takes the water to pene-

trate the predetermined depth (see page 102). And third, turn the irrigation system on and frequently check the area for water runoff. Always check a soil's moisture before deep watering.

In early fall, deep watering is ill advised on slopes. Debris flow, soil slips, and landslides increase in likelihood as soil reaches its water-saturation point. The goal of water in early fall is to keep the plants from drying out.

How to Calculate Deep Watering

To determine the amount of water a particular plant needs, you need to identify the type of soil around the plant and the plant's approximate rooting depth. After the soil type and rooting depth are known, a watering goal can be established. The information in this section explains how to identify soil types, gives general rooting depths, provides watering goals, and then provides the approximate time it takes reach the watering goals.

Soil Types and Their Characteristics

A landscape's soil type will influence not only the amount of water required, but also the most efficient irrigation system and the preferred type of plants. Determining the type of soil is important. It's also easy with the following steps:

1. Dig up two samples each of soil at three different depths: topsoil, 8 inches deep, and 20 inches deep.
2. Moisten one sample and let the other dry.
3. In your hands, cup and firmly squeeze the two samples.
4. Compare the samples to the characteristics listed below:

Soil Characteristics	Description
• **Coarse/Sand**	Soil is loose and easily falls apart, wet or dry.
• **Medium/Silt**	Dry, crumbles; moist, reluctantly retains its shape.
• **Fine/Clay**	Dry, breaks into clumps; wet, easily holds shape.

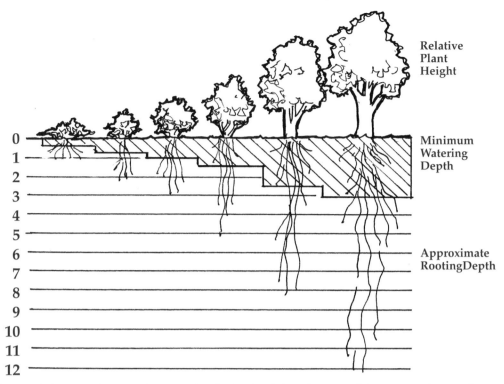

Illustrated above are the approximate rooting depths for six broad groups of plants: ground covers (low and high), shrubs (low and high), and trees (low and high). *Source: Adapted* from Low Volume Landscape Irrigation Design Manual, *Rain Bird Sales Inc. Contractor Division, 1994.*

orates. Each plant has specific needs and will consume water based on its rooting depth, its leaf surface area, and its transpiration (evaporation) rates. Humidity, wind, and temperature also affect the ability of both plants and soil to use and retain water. The information below is based on averages, and no soil is average.

The most important rule to keep in mind is that a soil's ability to absorb water is always greatest within its top 2 inches. Water infiltration is quicker at first and then dramatically tapers off, especially in denser soils. If water is given at a rate greater than a soil's ability to absorb it, the soil's pores fill with tiny particles, causing infiltration to almost stop. Patience is the key to deep watering.

Approximate Rooting Depths

The illustration above provides watering goals for six general plant groups. Seventy percent of the water a plant takes in comes from the top half of its root zone. This top half is the minimum watering depth (mwd) for the plant group. The root zone is the entire depth and width of a plant's roots.

Watering Times

It is difficult to apply a generalized model to any one situation. The amount of water any plant or landscape needs depends on many variables. A soil's structure and texture influence the amount of water it holds and evap-

While the goal is to get water to at least 50 percent of the root zone, this goal may not always be feasible, or even desirable. Many fire-prone landscapes sit upon bedrock and do not have deep soils. If there is only 2 feet of soil, there's no sense trying to get water to 3 feet. And lastly, the deep and infrequent method is not ideal for productive landscapes. This method can stress some plants, because it causes extremes in wet and dry. Landscapes that are designed for high productivity will require a more consistent level of moisture.

The watering times in the chart below are used for dry soils. Moist or wet soils should be allowed to dry before using the recommendations listed. Under each type of plant group is its "preferred minimum watering depth" (pmwd); pmwd is the top 75 percent of a plant's root zone and the ideal depth that water should go to create healthy, deeply rooted plants.

Watering Systems

Water-dependent gardens are directly linked to the water's distribution system. The type and condition of a watering system can affect a landscape's maintenance costs and risk of fire. A properly picked and maintained water system will help create a healthy, fire-retardant landscape.

Before designing and installing an irrigation system, several points should be considered:

Keep the irrigation system simple. The more moving parts, sprinkler heads, and corners a system has, the higher its installation and maintenance costs.

Try to keep plants of similar needs on one line: ground covers with ground covers, shrubs with shrubs, and so forth. As groups are mixed, the range of problems increases.

Budget time and money for irrigation maintenance. The calendar in Chapter 9 provides timely tasks that will help keep a system efficient.

Plants come and go, but some irrigation systems can stick around. A well-maintained system can last more than 20 years. Longevity is ensured when new planting plans are designed around the existing system, instead of always trying to force the system to adapt to the plants.

An irrigation system that will be used as part of the emergency watering system will need to be modified. To compensate for the dramatic

Watering Times			
Plant Group pmwd	**Coarse/Sand**	**Medium/Silt**	**Fine/Clay**
As shown below, deep watering is time consuming. Fortunately, soils that are slow to take water are also slow to lose it. Even in the middle of summer, it may take three to four weeks for clay soils to dry. (Note: gpm is gallons per minute. Also, 1 inch of water equals 62 gallons of water, the equivalent of filling 100 square feet with 1 inch of water.)			
Low, shallow-rooted ground covers 3 inches	Water: 0.25"/15 gal. Time: 1–2 min./10 gpm max. pressure	Water: 0.375"/23 gal. Time: 4–5 min./6 gpm. max. pressure	Water: 0.5"/31 gal. Time: 8 min./4 gpm max. pressure
Medium-sized ground covers 6 inches	Water: 0.5"/31 gal. Time: 4–5 min./7.75 gpm max. pressure	Water: 0.75"/46 gal. Time: 13 min./3.5 gpm max. pressure	Water: 1"/62 gal. Time: 1 hr./1 gpm max. pressure
Large ground covers 9 inches	Water: 0.75"/46 gal. Time: 12 min./4 gpm max. pressure	Water: 1.25"/77 gal. Time: 25 min./3 gpm max. pressure	Water: 1.5"/93 gal. Time: 1.5 hrs./1 gpm max. pressure
Small shrubs 1.5 feet	Water: 1.5"/93 gal. Time: 26 min./3.5 gpm max. pressure	Water: 2.25"/140 gal. Time: 48 min./3 gpm max. pressure	Water: 3"/186 gal. Time: 3 hrs./1 gpm max. pressure
Large shrubs 2.25 feet	Water: 2.25"/140 gal. Time: 42 min./3 gpm max. pressure	Water: 3.375"/232 gal. Time: 1.25 hrs./3 gpm max. pressure	Water: 4.5"/279 gal. Time: 4 hrs. 50 min./0.9 gpm max. pressure
Small trees 3 feet	Water: 3"/186 gal. Time: 1 hr. 6 min./2.8 gpm max. pressure	Water: 4.5"/209 gal. Time: 1 hr. 45 min./2.8 gpm max. pressure	Water: 6.5"/403 gal. Time: 7 hrs. 10 min./0.8 gpm max. pressure
Large trees 3.75 feet	Water: 3.75"/232 gal. Time: 1 hr. 36 min./2.4 gpm max. pressure	Water: 5.625"/349 gal. Time: 2 hrs. 26 min./2.4 gpm max. pressure	Water: 7.5"/465 gal. Time: 8 hrs. 33 min./0.8 gpm max. pressure

Source: Adapted from Estimating Water Requirements of Landscape Plantings: The Landscape Coefficient Method, *Cooperative Extension University of California, Division of Agriculture and Natural Resources, Leaflet 21493; and* Low Volume Landscape Irrigation Design Manual, *Rain Bird Sales Inc. Contractor Division, 1994.*

drop in water pressure during a wildfire, an irrigation line should use only 55 percent of the line's available water. An irrigation specialist can help design an effective emergency watering system.

Four commonly used irrigation systems are described below and evaluated on their best uses, advantages, and disadvantages. Helpful hints are also included to improve each system's efficiency.

High Volume: PVC Pipe Sprinkler Systems

Typically run underground, high-pressure watering systems are long lasting, low maintenance, and typically made from polyvinyl chloride, or PVC, pipe. Attached to this durable pipe are impulse, pop-up, and rotational sprinkler heads.

Generally, high-pressure systems never water one plant; they water a large area. Overhead sprinkler systems are ideal for densely planted areas, areas with low ground covers, and coarse soils. These sprinkler systems provide quick and reliable application of water, which makes them ideal for emergency sprinkler systems.

The disadvantages of these common systems are well known: They are not the most efficient water users; water loss is common from evaporation, runoff, and overspray. These systems can also create over- and underwatered plants.

Although high-pressure sprinkler systems are considered low maintenance, they are in reality just more forgiving of maintenance neglect, unlike the drip system. Changing or repairing these systems can be expensive because of the high labor costs. Puddles and runoff

This picture is a common sight. Over- and underspray are common problems with high-pressure watering systems.

are common when a plant grows in front of a sprinkler head's spray.

Tips: At the beginning of each sprinkler line, install a shut-off valve, a filter, and screwable unions. By making each line completely independent, a station can be taken apart without affecting another line's performance. Sprinkler lines near foot traffic should be built with schedule 40 PVC pipe, and swing joints should be installed at each sprinkler head, making individual adjustments easier and minimizing the chance of breakage.

High Volume: Hose Ends

Hose-end sprinkler systems offer the same advantages as the PVC system, but water is provided by screw-on sprinkler heads attached to common garden hoses. This inexpensive, high-pressure system is typically run above ground. Hose ends are easy to assemble and install.

Hose-end sprinklers are used to establish a garden that will be weaned off supplemental water once established. They are also used for seasonal gardens and on slopes, where digging is not advised. Hose ends require regular replacement of hoses if used permanently. They are also unstable and easily disturbed. These systems have all the disadvantages as other high-pressure systems: water loss from evaporation, runoff, leaks, and overspray.

Tips: To prevent leaks, use plumber's tape to cover the threads of all unions that screw together. Use longer-lasting brass fittings instead of plastic. Place mulch over the hose to protect it from aging. To anchor the sprinkler heads, tie them to a stake, pipe, or rebar that has been hammered deep into the ground. Avoid leaving the water on while the sprinkler heads are turned off, as unreleased pressure will cause a hose to prematurely rupture.

Low Volume: Drip Systems

Drip systems are low-flow water systems. These watering devices are considered water wise because they provide water at the rate a soil can absorb it. Using relatively less water over an extended period of time is the most effective way to get water deeper into the ground and to encourage a plant's roots to grow deep. This system delivers water at or below a planted surface.

Drip system is a term used to describe a wide variety of water systems. It is typically made from black polyethylene plastic. Water is dispersed by emitters, small sprinkler heads, and mister heads. Drip systems cater to the individual needs of plants.

Deep-rooting plants, planted slopes, windy environments, landscapes that are sensitive to high humidity, and containers can benefit from the advantages of a low-flow system. These systems direct water away from the base of woody plants and non-planted areas, lowering the chances of rot and weeds.

A drip system is not low maintenance. The small heads are easily clogged and kicked over. The thin hoses deteriorate faster than PVC and are more prone to accidental damage, by such things as snow and rodents. In coarse soils, more heads will be needed to water a bed, because water's horizontal movement is minimal. Also, isolated islands of water, as opposed to complete coverage, can affect the health of microorganisms in the soil.

Tips: Installing and regularly cleaning water filters is the single most important task. Particle-free water extends the life of the small drip heads. To keep minerals from building up in the tubing, uncap the end of each water line and flush them with water for two minutes. Flushing a system is an annual task, typical done at the end of March. To keep the tubing from becoming brittle, partially bury exposed pipe. Mark buried tubing so it is not accidentally cut or kicked.

Low Volume: Soaker Tubing and In-Line Tubing

Soaker tubing and in-line emitter tubing enjoy all the benefits of the low-flow philosophy. Like drip systems, they provide water at the rate a soil can absorb it and they promote deeply rooted plants. Soaker hoses are made from water-permeable plastic and ooze water along their length. In-line tubing has small holes along its length. This low-flow watering device can be connected to any type of irrigation system or faucet.

Soaker tubing is affected by environmental elements more than any other type of irrigation system. Leaks, stiff sections, and uneven water distribution are common problems as they deteriorate. Laying a soaker hose over uneven ground can also cause uneven water distribution. As fine particles fill their holes, in-line tubing can also create unwanted water patterns.

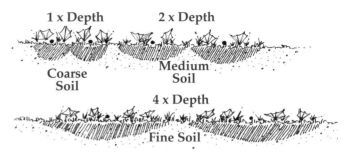

The denser the soil gets, the further away emitters and soaker tubing can be placed. As a general rule, the desired depth is equal to the emitter spacing distance in coarse soils, two times in medium soil, and four times the depth in fine soils. For example, deep watering to 6 inches means putting the emitters 6 inches, 1 foot, or 2 feet apart, in sand, silt, and clay soils, respectively.

Tips: Level the ground before laying out the soaker tubing. To protect the tubing and hoses from the elements, partially bury them. As with all irrigation systems, install and regularly clean water filters. Most soaker hoses have screwable end-caps and should be flushed annually.

Watering on Slopes

Deep watering slopes is tough: Water infiltration rates are low, runoff is likely, and water tends to accumulate at the bottom. The chart and illustration that follow will help. The chart provides a starting point for determining how fast a soil can take water; it aids in determining the type of irrigation system. Recommendations for sprinkler head placement are given in the illustration below.

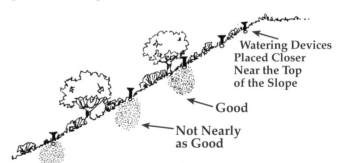

Above are recommendations for sprinkler head placement.

In-line tubing and emitters are preferred on slopes. With a main supply line running up a slope, connect the horizontal tubing. All emitters should be pressure-compensating, so that flow will be even throughout the area. Tubing is spaced 24 inches apart in clay soil and 12 inches apart in sandy soil. Because of the downward movement of water, tubing should always be placed closer together at the top of a hill. The distance between heads increases down the

Maximum Precipitation Rates

Maximum Precipitation Rate (MPR) is a starting point for accurately determining how fast a particular slope can absorb water. These rates are given in inches per hour and gallons of water per hour (gph), per 4 square feet. Loam is a reference to organic material in a soil. Slopes with vegetation growing on them can absorb water at a greater rate than those that do not have vegetation, hence the two listings, accounting for a cover or a bare slope. To convert percentage of slope to degrees, see Chapter 10. Lastly, remember that the values below are averages, and no slope or soil is average.

% of Slope	Coarse/ Sand	Sandy Loam	Medium/ Silt	Fine/ Clay
0–5%	Cover: 2" at 5 gph Bare: 2" at 4.3 gph	Cover: 1.75" at 4.3 gph Bare: 1"/2.5 gph	Cover: 1" at 2.5 gph Bare: 0.5" at 1.25 gph	Cover: 0.2" at 0.5 gph Bare: 0.15" at 0.37 gph
5–8%	Cover: 2" at 5 gph Bare: 1.5" at 3.75 gph	Cover: 1.25" at 3 gph Bare: 0.8" at 2 gph	Cover: 0.8" at 2 gph Bare: 0.4" at 1 gph	Cover: 0.15" at 0.37 gph Bare: 0.1" at 0.25 gph
8–12%	Cover: 1.5" at 3.75 gph Bare: 1" at 2.5 gph	Cover: 1" at 2.5 gph Bare: 0.6" at 1.5 gph	Cover: 0.6" at 1.5 gph Bare: 0.3" at 0.75 gph	Cover: 0.12" at 0.3 gph Bare: .08" at 0.2 gph
12%–up	Cover: 1" at 2.5 gph Bare: 0.5" at 1.25 gph	Cover: 0.75" at 1.86 gph Bare: 0.4" at 1 gph	Cover: 0.4" at 1 gph Bare: 0.2" at 0.5 gph	Cover: 0.1" at 0.25 gph Bare: 0.06" at 0.15 gph

Source: Adapted from Landscape Irrigation Design Manual, *Rain Bird Sprinkler Manufacturing Corp., 2000; and* Drip Irrigation: For Every Landscape and All Climates, *by Robert Kourik Metamorphic Press, 1992.*

hill. All watering devices should be placed uphill of a plant. The soil in terraced beds tends to absorb water more quickly, and tubing will have to be placed closer together.

An excellent reference on low-volume irrigation systems is a book called *Drip Irrigation: For Every Landscape and Climate*, by Robert Kourik (Metamorphic Press, 1992).

Water Conservation

Water conservation plays a large role in a firescaped garden. Saving water extends a water budget, helps raise moisture levels in plants, and builds up water reserves for an emergency. The subject of water conservation is vast, but the basic principles are below:

Pick the Right Plant

The perfect plant will not only save water, it will be low maintenance, effective in its function, and it will look good—not always easily found. Sometimes finding it takes time, but it's time definitely well spent. Chapter 7 was designed to make the most of water conservation and fire safety. There is a perfect plant.

Plant in Groups

Grouping plants according to their needs is the key to any successful garden. Plants with specific water, sun, nutrient, and maintenance needs should always be grown together. These groupings create healthier plants and concentrate resource and maintenance costs, saving money, time, and water.

Mulch

The benefits of laying out mulch are well known. Top-dressing slows water evaporation, suppresses weed growth, and slows water runoff and erosion. Mulching is an integral part of a healthy garden. A cautionary note: Finely shredded mulches are flammable and known to ignite. Chipped mulches are less ignitable.

Maintain

Haphazard maintenance of irrigation systems wastes millions of gallons of water a year. Leaky unions should be fixed, filters cleaned, lines flushed, heads adjusted, and timers fine-tuned in a water-conscious landscape.

Weed and Prune

Any type of excess vegetation, whether or not it comes from an unwanted plant, should be removed. Weeding and pruning lowers the leaf surface area of a landscape, which saves water and lowers the amount of fuels.

Use Less Fertilizer

Although they can improve health, fertilizers are stimulants, and along with boosting plant growth, they increase the need for water. Fertilizers should be used only to fix nutrient deficiencies. Constantly mulching a landscape, as recommended above, may provide all the nutrients necessary to sustain a landscape's health.

Simply Use Less Water

How long does it take for plants to wilt and soils to dry? How much water is needed to recharge the soil and how long will it take? If the answers to these questions are unknown, the landscape is probably overwatered. The only way to get this valuable information is to stop watering.

Emergency Water

An emergency watering system has two goals. First, it must raise the ignition tolerance (the amount of time and heat that are required to ignite) of the house and landscape. Secondly, it must help extinguish incoming firebrands as well as the small fires they create. A good system serves these two goals, while remaining effective during severe wildfire conditions.

Two events are likely to occur during a wildfire: a dramatic drop in water pressure and the complete loss of electric power. An emergency system will compensate for these two possibilities. Properties in high elevations and rural areas are more prone to these two problems, and their emergency water system will have to be independent of the municipal water and power supply.

Designing an Emergency Water-Delivery System

An emergency water-delivery system should be designed for versatility and ease of use. Sprinkler heads

Perspectives: Marie Carr-Fitzgerald, Vice President of Shasta County Historical Society, Redding

I live near the Coleman Fish Hatchery, 8 miles east of Cottonwood, across the Sacramento River. I live in the Battle Creek valley—it is very green and lush. We have some valley oaks, some blue oak, not much manzanita here; there is a lot of dry grass. And in the summer, sometimes we've had it in the 118s and 120s. Doesn't stay that way, but it's hot and dry.

Our community has grown. It is gradually turning from rural cattle and farming, and some of it is being sold off for homes. Not much business, yet. There are not a lot of springs or creeks. Even in our country, the land prices are going up, depending on if you've got water or what you're buying. They've doubled, and in some cases, tripled in price. And development is catching up.

We haven't had fire through our particular area, but it has been around us. There was the Fountain fire, and then they've had quite a few fires in the Trinity Alps area, which is on the west side of us. And then we had one that was up by Shasta Lake, which was quite severe and burned a lot of homes.

There are times and places when a fire is good for an area. I know we have great marshes with cattails, and it would probably be really helpful if those places would be burnt off every once in awhile to give something else a chance to grow in there. Fires have their place, but they do need to be controlled. You just can't say you'll burn off something and then hope for the best.

are installed to raise the ignition tolerance of plants and roofs. Hoses are used to extinguish flying sparks and flames. The sprinkler heads are used when a fire is a great distance away, and the hoses as the fire approaches.

An emergency water-delivery system that is connected to a municipal water supply will have to compensate for the potential loss of water pressure. The sprinkler system should be able to remain effective with a 55 percent drop in water pressure. This simply means fewer sprinkler heads for each water line.

Whether a water-delivery system will work may never be known until it is needed. Always build a system using the highest quality materials: Brass fittings should be used instead of plastic, and galvanized steel pipe is preferable to PVC. Regularly testing and oiling all moving parts, such as sprinkler heads, will help create a system that is always ready.

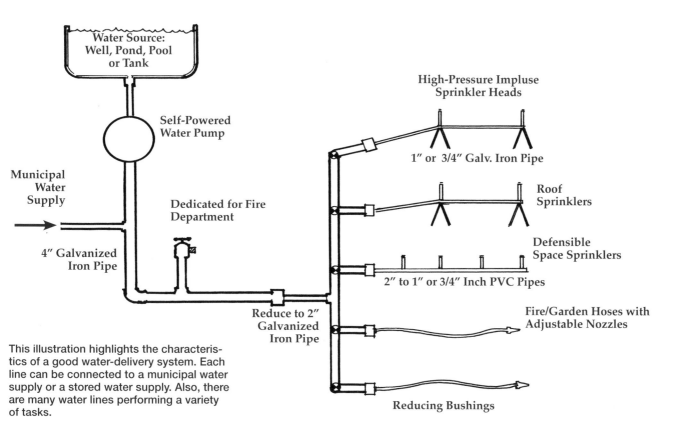

This illustration highlights the characteristics of a good water-delivery system. Each line can be connected to a municipal water supply or a stored water supply. Also, there are many water lines performing a variety of tasks.

Emergency Water Sources

Although any amount of stored water can make a difference in combating a blaze, the more water a property has, the better. Most fire departments recommend at least 1,000 gallons of stored emergency water. A water source over 1,000 gallons should be brought to the fire department's attention. Firefight-

This rooftop sprinkler is designed to wet and cool the roof and deck below. This sprinkler will be effective during a wildfire because it is the only head on the line and is made from the highest-quality materials, a brass head and galvanized steel pipe.

ers are more likely to stop at a structure if they know they have water to defend it. Some fire departments issue blue identification reflectors that help identify a water source from the road.

Emergency water can be stored in a variety of ways. Hot tubs, ponds, cisterns, and water tanks are all excellent sources of emergency water, but each requires different accessories to make water retrievable. Below are the characteristics that enable these sources to provide water in an emergency:

Hot Tubs, Pools, and Spas: These common outdoor features are ideal sources of emergency water. They typically have great access, their drainage systems are easy to use, and their water is rarely as dirty as the water in ponds. An emergency water pump and fire hose are necessary accessories.

Ponds: Most naturally occurring ponds are dry in the summer, and if they are wet, much of the bottom water is unusable because of the large amount of debris. Turning a pond into an effective water source requires at least 2 feet of clear water above the murkiness. Any water pump used to retrieve a pond's water should have a fine-meshed screen over its water intake. A long suction hose, up to 8-foot suction, also will be needed. A gas-powered water pump is frequently used to retrieve water from a pond.

Water Tanks and Cisterns: Common in high-elevation areas, properties with water wells, and water-scarce neighborhoods, water tanks are an excellent source of emergency water. These sometimes large structures can be made from redwood, plastic, fiberglass, or concrete. Cisterns, which are underground water tanks, are fairly expensive.

In most cases, a water tank is used to supply the domestic water needs of a property. Emergency water is any water in the tank at the time of an emergency. To ensure that there will always be water for an emergency, design a water tank's plumbing from the illustration below.

Access and Plumbing Guidelines for Stored Water

Many people living in fire-prone areas do not have water pumps or electric generators, and cannot retrieve their water for emergency purposes. Creating access and outfitting a water supply with the proper plumbing will aid the firefighters' efforts to get to and use the stored water.

A water source should be 200 feet from the area where firefighters will park their trucks. On hills, the water source should be 50 feet from where firefighters will park. No matter how far the water source, an easy-to-use pathway should be created and maintained. Perhaps most importantly, the area immediately around a water source should have only well-kept trees and shrubs. Firefighters must be able to lay fire hoses in all directions.

Water sources with drain pipes, such as pools and water tanks, can be inexpensively modified to make their fittings compatible with a firefighter's hose. A 2.5-inch threaded male fitting installed on a drain pipe makes it compatible with the hoses that firefighters use. An adapting bushing can then be screwed on top of the male fitting to accommodate a garden hose and every day use. All open water sources should have a water

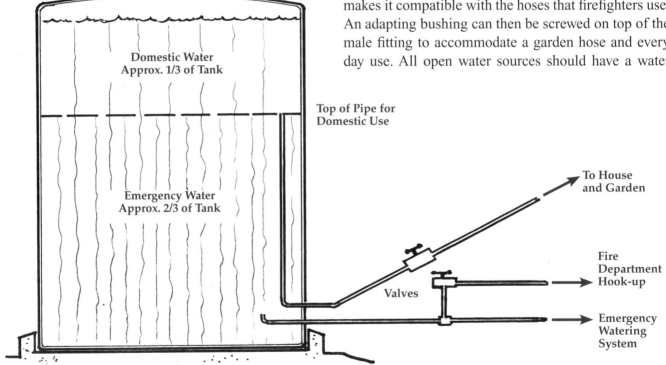

Keeping the pipe for domestic water use well above a tank's halfway point will ensure that there is always water for an emergency.

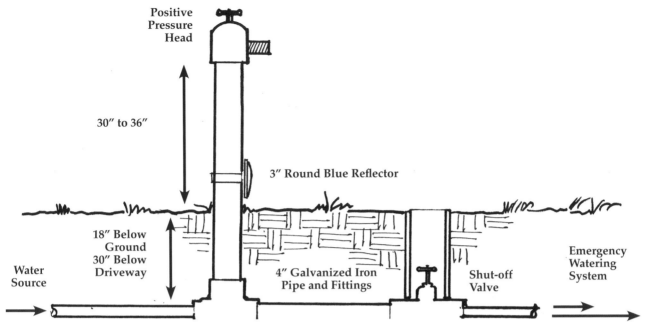

The hoses firefighters use need special fittings to work on a residential property. These special characteristics are called out in the illustration above.

filter installed before drainage pipes and water pumps. Hoses and pumps can be clogged by debris that naturally settles to the bottom.

Water Pumps and Hoses

With a lack of electricity and/or a big drop in water pressure, a good water pump can become critical in defending a structure against a wildfire. For emergency purposes, there are two types of pumps to shop for: an electrical water pump and a gasoline-powered water pump.

An electrical water pump may require a separate electric generator to keep it running during an emergency. Ideally, electric pumps are installed near the drain pipes of pools, spas, and water tanks.

Gasoline-powered water pumps are the type used by firefighters. Although gasoline-powered pumps are more expensive than electric, they are invaluable if there has been a power failure, or if the water source is a long distance away. Purchase a pump that can be carried and handled by one person.

A pump that delivers water at 100 gallons per minute (gpm) and at 50 pounds per square inch of pressure (psi) is recommended for home protection. A 250 gpm, 100 psi pump is preferred to retrieve and distribute water from large water-storage tanks. Pumps that deliver 50 gpm are available and purchased for small storages. All water pumps should be purchased with an 8-foot suction hose, 100 feet of fire hose, and an adjustable fire nozzle. A fire hose is distinguished by its fire-resistant cotton jacket.

All generators, pumps, and hoses should be well maintained. Gasoline-powered generators and pumps should be oiled and tested regularly, especially at the beginning of each fire season. Fire hoses should be kept out of the sun, away from excess moisture, and protected from chewing bugs and animals. An emergency water system has to be in excellent operating order, not for one or two fire seasons, but for the life of the structure it is meant to protect.

Chapter 9

Maintaining a Firescaped Garden

Every plant, every garden, and every house is flammable. The degree of their flammability is directly related to the maintenance they receive. Poor designs, due to either plant selection or architectural elements, can increase the fire risk, but more often than not, lack of maintenance leads a fire to a house.

Pruning, removing, and watering plants are the biggest contributors to a garden's health and fire safety. These maintenance chores affect a landscape's potential flammability in four distinct ways:

Proximity to potential sources of fire, such as roads, open spaces, work areas, and chimneys, greatly affects a landscape's chances of ignition. The fuels surrounding and leading away from these ignition areas determine the amount of risk they pose.

Ignitability, a combination of temperature and conditions that are required to make the landscape burst into flames, is influenced by a landscape's type of vegetation, its moisture content, and its amount of deadwood.

Combustibility of a landscape—the amount of heat it produces when on fire—is related to the landscape's type of vegetation. A lot of the wrong plants, such as pine trees, can increase a landscape's combustibility and its ability to rapidly spread the fire.

Sustainability—the ability of a landscape to keep a fire going—is changed by altering a landscape's structure, density, and moisture content. The more fuel a landscape has, the longer it can feed a fire.

A fire-retardant garden is never created just once, it is maintained over a lifetime. Wildfires may take the colder months off, but they are a genuine threat the rest of the year. Our landscapes must be able to protect us for the greater portion of the year, every year. They almost always have to be ready: On any windy day, wildfires can spot a neglected property from miles away.

Maintaining a fire-protected property requires a schedule of tasks, priorities for these tasks, and a honest evaluation of the amount of time and money that an individual can spend on these tasks. This chapter includes a list that prioritizes tasks, calendars that highlight the best time of year to perform these tasks, and a section on pruning, which is critical to maintaining a firescaped garden.

Maintenance Priorities

After competing with life's many demands, what little time is left for the garden usually has to be prioritized. In a firescaped garden, work is done around the house first, then downhill, and lastly, towards the direction of summer's dangerous winds, which blow toward the ocean. The following maintenance tasks are prioritized first to save a family, then to save a home, and third, to protect the garden.

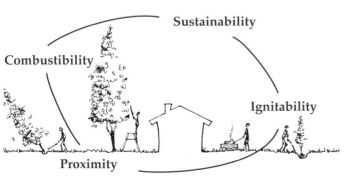

The four factors of flammability illustrated above are greatly influenced by the amount or lack of maintenance.

Perspectives: Adam Rowe, Owner of Custom Landscapes, Rough and Ready

We're living in the foothills of Sierra Nevada. It's been years since any major conflagration—the 49er fire raged through acres and acres, clear down to Lake Wildwood, actually, all the way down to Bridgeport. People could potentially settle into complacency but are fairly diligent. They do what they can; they do what they can afford.

It's a lot of weed-whacking and maintaining. The fire department wants a green band around the house. You can opt not to have any vegetation at all. Some people weed-whack it to the ground and there's nothing there to burn. You must have a fuel break. [Fire officials] come every year and give you a "yea" or "nay."

The more remote a place is . . . I just think it's harder. We're a half mile from a fire station, and [there are] 30 homes on the road. [Twelve years ago], the homeowners banded together and there was a big of effort to protect each other [from wildfire]. Chainsaws came from everywhere.

If you weed-whack before the last of the rains, [the weeds] grow back so strong and you [have to] do it again, which is fine for certain areas. But if you want to do a particular area just once, then you wait until the last of the rains when the grass goes to seed. When we first moved here, we were talking to the neighbors about weed-whacking and when do they do it. They said that they wait for [another neighbor] Jerry to do it. When he comes out, it's time, and the next two weeks everybody is running their weed-whackers.

One thing I've noticed about folks who move from the city is that they are used to having the immediate area around them landscaped, but what they are not used to is the amount of square footage that is your immediate area up here. Easily, you can put too much of your landscaping budget into the immediate surroundings and not have enough for the greater area.

Maintain a Path for Exit

Any individual should be able to move easily throughout a property, without ducking, tripping, or worrying about what's ahead. On larger lots, making and maintaining two exits is essential. Maintaining a safe exit may mean pruning low-hanging limbs, removing aggressive ground covers, and repairing steps and handrails. A safe exit is essential in any emergency, not just in fires.

Clean Around the House

Remove all plant litter from immediately around the house. From underneath eaves, decks, and vents, remove stored newspapers, wood piles, and any plant that has grown up and under these overhangs. Clean the roof. Sweep off leaves, clean the rain gutters, put spark arresters on chimneys and stove pipes, and remove tree limbs 8 feet past the roof line and 10 feet beyond chimneys.

Maintain Zone 1

Remove all litter and dead plant material within 30 feet of a house. Cut all non-ornamental grasses down to 6 inches. Remove the lower limbs of mature trees and clear around younger ones. Mature trees should have their lower branches removed 8 feet from the ground. Young and adolescent trees should have flammable material and combustible ground covers removed at least 2 feet past their drip lines. Remove dense plantings and other fuels at least 10 feet away from the drip lines of mature trees.

Remove aggressive vines, such as ivy, honeysuckle, and poison oak, from trees and shrubs. Remove loose bark and companion plants, such as mistletoe and Spanish moss, from shrubs and trees. Break continuous lines of vegetation from potential sources of fire, such as roads, open spaces, and work areas.

Clean Around the Driveway

Remove trees and shrubs 6 feet past the paved surface. Remove litter. Maintain the paths that lead to a house. Provide a place for vehicles to turn around.

Clear the Road to a House

Roads, driveways, and paths are firebreaks. If these urban features are maintained properly, they can stop or dramatically slow a fire. Firefighters will also make a stand on roads, and they choose them carefully; a well-maintained firebreak will invite firefighters.

Overhanging branches provide a pathway for a fire and obstruct emergency vehicles. Make sure the address and street signs are clearly visibility. Remove trees and shrubs 6 feet from either side of a road. Prune branches that overhang a road up to 16 feet. Ask the power company to prune or remove trees growing into power lines. Keep wild grasses down to 6 inches high.

Clear and Thin Zones 2 and 3

Remove flammable vegetation around liquid propane gas tanks, additional structures, wood piles, and power poles. Remove litter and dead plant material. Thin and isolate shrubs by two times their height and trees by three times their drip lines. Keep flammable plants 10 feet from the drip lines of trees.

Help Your Community

No garden is an island, and your best efforts can easily be thwarted by a neighbor's indifference. In many cases, good neighborly relations and community participation are mandatory to protect homes from a wildfire.

Weather Calendar

Many plants are pruned in February and March because of the low likelihood of a hard frost. But it is not the month that dictates pruning in late winter/early spring, it is the weather. The tasks listed in the following calendar are all weather contingent. As a particular climate or microclimate changes, the timing of tasks is adjusted accordingly. California's average weather pattern is illustrated below.

Maintenance Calendar	Jan.	Feb.	Mar.	April	May	June	July	Aug.	Sept.	Oct.	Nov.	Dec.
Prune: Conifers			▬	▬	▬							
Deciduous		▬	▬	▬						▬	▬	▬
Summer Flowering		▬	▬	▬								
Spring Flowering				▬	▬	▬						
Suckers		▬	▬									
Watersprouts								▬	▬			
Pinch			▬	▬								
Thin							▬	▬				
Maintenance: Clean Storm Drain	▬	▬	▬									
Remove Dead Wood					▬	▬						
Clean Wind Damage								▬	▬			
Erosion Control	▬									▬	▬	▬
Fix Irrigation			▬	▬								
Weeding		▬ Heavy	▬	▬			▬ Light	▬	▬			
Mulch		▬	▬	▬					▬	▬		
Water			▬ Light	▬	▬	▬ Light and Infrequent	▬	▬	▬	▬ Very Light	▬	▬
1st Water			Lawns		Ivy	Herbs		Citrus	Citrus			
Plant	Bareroot & Bulbs			Sensitive Plants				Transplants & Cuttings		All Other Plants		
Storm Cycle	⚡	⚡	⚡	☀	☀	☀	☀	☀	☀	⚡	⚡	⚡
Fire Season						▬	▬	▬	▬	▬		

Make and maintain community greenbelts—low-growing, irrigated pastures—around any group of houses. Plants selected for greenbelts are from the zone 2 plants list. Make or maintain community pathways, emergency roads, and private roads. Thin and weed zone 4, which is typically shared by a community. All of this will create firebreaks. Also, support education and action through community associations and neighborhood groups.

Monthly Checklist

Proper timing of tasks is essential to the goals of firescaping. Out-of-season maintenance can either encourage or create fires. The effects of pests, storms, and water shortages can be greatly reduced by performing basic, scheduled tasks.

The weather calendar (page 113) and the month-by-month calendar that follows in this section highlight the most important tasks for a firescaped garden. The first is a graph that illustrates all the work that is weather dependent. The second calendar is a month-by-month checklist. However, a garden's maintenance costs and chances of ignition can be lowered by doing three common chores—clearing, planting, and pruning—at appropriate times.

Clearing land and removing plants should be done in late winter to early spring. Most plants have not produced seed yet and there may be several months of mild rain left, which will nourish the soil and remaining plants.

Planting in the fall saves water, time, and money. Fall-planted plants are more resilient to summer's heat and can able be weaned off supplemental water more quickly. Naturally, the exceptions to this rule are in the mountains.

Prune trees, shrubs, and ground covers when they will recover the quickest. Every plant has its own unique cycle. Pruning that appreciates these cycles is much more effective. The pruning calendar on page 119 takes these cycles into account.

January
In the Garden

- Assess the goals of the landscape and develop a plan to reach those goals.
- Remove deadwood created by storms.

- Prune and spray dormant plants, except those that flower early.
- Buy and plant bare-root plants, such as grapes, roses, and fruit trees.
- Clean, sharpen, and replace tools.
- Look for bargains at garden centers.
- Turn the compost pile.

Emergency Preparedness

- List items needed in an emergency, and go out and get them.
- Make a list of phone numbers needed in an emergency.

February
In the Garden

- Look for signs and immediately fix water problems, such as puddling or runoff, which cause rills and gullies. Solutions to erosion and drainage problems are offered in Chapter 10.
- Finish spraying or pruning dormant trees and shrubs, except those that flower early.
- Prune roses and grapes.
- Prevent soil compaction by not walking on garden beds until dry, which can take weeks with clay soils.
- Mulch heavily to suppress weeds.
- Plant summer-flowering bulbs, such as anemone, gladiolus, and tuber begonias.
- Control the early emergence of snails and slugs.
- Control diseases, like peach curl, from last year with either copper or sulfur fungicides.
- Look for bargains at garden centers.

Emergency Preparedness

- Pack an emergency kit: radio, first aid kit, flashlight, and three days' worth of water and food.
- Familiarize yourself with local fire codes.

March
In the Garden

- Begin planting in the mountain areas.
- Flush, test, and fix irrigation systems.
- Mow and remove the dead interior of ground covers (de-thatch), such as ivy, hypericum, cape weed, periwinkle, and wild strawberry.

- Reinvigorate lawns by de-thatching, seeding, fertilizing, and mulching.
- Generously apply mulch throughout garden.
- Divide and prune perennials.
- Finish planting summer-blooming bulbs.
- Pull weeds before they can set seed.
- Begin pruning spring-flowering trees and shrubs, such as ceanothus, forsythia, lilac, and viburnum.
- Fertilize productive, domestic landscapes with a high-nitrogen mixture.

Emergency Preparedness

- Check visibility of street name and addresses.
- Volunteer time and money to community cleanup and fuel-removal programs.

April
In the Garden

- Reclaim 30 feet of defensible space around the house.
- Continue planting in mountains; start planting frost-sensitive plants.
- Control and guide the flush of spring growth.
- Iron deficiencies are the most obvious right now; fix with either a foliar spray or longer-lasting chelated iron.
- Aphid and snail populations swell; treat as necessary.
- Black spot, sooty mold, rust, and mildew begin to grow again along the coast. Prune out the worst infestations and remove surrounding vegetation to increase sunlight and air circulation. Use fungicides as a last resort.
- Plant transplants of summer annuals and vegetables.
- Prune spring-flowering trees and shrubs, such as ceanothus, forsythia, lilac, and viburnum.
- Last good chance to sow wildflower seeds.
- Pick the first strawberry.

Emergency Preparedness

- Call your local fire station and ask for an inspection of the landscape. Having emergency personnel visit a property prior to an emergency will help everyone during any type of emergency.
- Pull together and/or update important docments that will be needed in case you have to flee your home.

May
In the Garden

- Keep defensible space clear.
- Only turn water system back on when soil is dry at least 1 foot down.
- Plant summer annuals and vegetables.
- Plant citrus trees.
- Cut non-ornamental grasses to 6 inches.
- Continue to prune spring-blooming shrubs, such as rhododendron.
- Domestic soils may be depleted after spring growth. Fertilize if nutrient deficiencies are visible.
- Sheer or tip plants to create hedges.

Emergency Preparedness

- Check and clean garden hoses, fire extinguishers, and auxiliary water pumps.
- Locate the gas shutoff valve and make sure its wrench is within reach of the valve.

June
In the Garden

- Begin watering at first signs of water stress.
- Clean up after mid-season fruit drop.
- Loosen the ties that support new trees.
- Protect new trees from sunburn by wrapping vulnerable areas with cloth.
- Monitor and prepare to combat swelling pest populations.
- Prune climbing roses.
- Raise the height of the lawn mower to 1 inch.
- Pick first wild berry.
- Stop watering native plants.

Emergency Preparedness

- Remove any type of ignitable debris around the house and garden.
- Demand that flammable neighbors comply with local fire codes.

July
In the Garden

- Native and Mediterranean gardens begin their period of rest, which means little or no water or pruning.
- Cut or pull out unwanted resprouting shrubs.
- Mulch zone 1 plants, especially those that are heat sensitive, like rhododendrons and camellias.
- Plant bougainvillea.
- Do not let the weeds go to seed.
- Watch for water stress.
- Control chewing worms.
- Solarize soil where desired.
- Take cuttings of perennials.
- Pick up after fruit trees.
- Good time to tackle construction projects.

Emergency Preparedness

- Lay out and hook up emergency equipment, such as hoses and shovels.
- Check ladders and then place close to the house, for easy access to the roof.

August
In the Garden

- Keep the landscape surrounding a house well watered and free of deadwood.
- Cut branches 10 feet past chimneys and stovepipes.
- Begin planting winter annuals and vegetables.
- Plant biennials, such as campanula and foxglove, by seed.
- Let late spring and summer flowers go to seed.
- Prepare a compost pile that will be ready for fall planting.

Emergency Preparedness

- Check and oil auxiliary water pumps and emergency generators.

September
In the Garden

- Clean roof and rain gutters.
- Keep the landscape surrounding a house well watered and free of deadwood.
- Clean fallen fruit and branches.

- Transplant seedlings.
- Prevent debris and leaves from building up to dangerous levels.
- Shop for plants.
- Fertilize domestic landscapes with a complete, low-dosage mixture, such as bone meal, guano, or poultry manure.
- Do not fertilize frost-sensitive plants in frost-prone areas.

Emergency Preparedness

- Continue to support community groups and their efforts to reduce fuels.
- With neighbors and/or professional, analyze drainage systems and develop remedies.

October
In the Garden

- For landscapes below 3,000 feet, the planting season begins for trees, shrubs, ground covers, perennials, spring-blooming bulbs, and cool-season annuals.
- Prune and divide perennials, such as daylilies, callas, yarrow, and salvias.
- Sow wildflower seeds.
- Keep the landscape surrounding a house well watered and free of deadwood.
- Prevent fallen, dried leaves from building up to dangerous levels.
- Overseed warm-season grasses.
- Start looking for snails and slugs again along the coast.
- Order bare-root plants.
- Clean storm drains and gutters. Begin preparing for rain and erosion.
- Prune certain trees, such as cottonwood, maple, and sycamore, preparing them winter.
- Severely cut lawns and then mulch.
- Aerate and mulch highly compacted parts of the garden, including footpaths and lawns.
- Let winter dormant plants, like roses, go to seed.
- Reduce watering.

Emergency Preparedness

- Conduct a fire drill.
- Keep vigilance over flammable debris around structures.

November

In the Garden

- **Continue fall planting.**
- **This is the last month to plant spring-flowering bulbs, such as hyacinth and tulips.**
- **Cast out wildflower seeds.**
  Lightly stake new trees or those with weak branches.
- **Prepare for wind and frost; insulate water and irrigation pipes from a freeze.**
- **Hire an arborist to evaluate the health of the trees in a landscape.**
- **Protect outdoor furniture and equipment.**
- **Clean annuals beds.**
- **Grab a fig.**
- **Turn off irrigation systems.**
- **Start a compost pile that will be ready for spring planting.**
- **Bare-root plants become available.**

Emergency Preparedness

- **Rent the California Department of Forestry and Fire Protection's *California Living Fire Safe* video.**

December

In the Garden

- **Protect tender plants from frost and wind.**
- **Severely prune scraggly perennials and biennials, such as sages, penstemon, grasses, daisies, and Matilija poppies.**
- **Apply dormant spray to deciduous plants.**
- **Employ erosion measures against severe rain.**
- **Weed. It's exceptionally easy this time of year.**
- **Turn the compost piles.**
- **Transplant dormant plants.**
- **Start shrubs from cuttings.**

Emergency Preparedness

- **Before decorating for the holidays, check and install smoke detectors.**
- **Check water in cut Christmas trees; live Christmas trees can tolerate only two weeks indoors.**

Pruning

The common thread running throughout all fire-prevention programs is fuel reduction. In a garden, this means pruning, and lots of it. Pruning is also as important to firescaping as it is to a garden's health and beauty. Fruit and flower production are enhanced, growth and direction are controlled, and beautiful shapes take form because of this seasonal chore.

Although reducing fuels is the most effective use of pruning time, once these fuels are removed, pruning on a regular basis will keep a garden safe and manageable. By lowering the leaf surface area of a plant, pruning conserves water, increases a plant's moisture content, and encourages new growth. New growth is moist, supple, and typically less vulnerable to insects and disease—all of which make a plant more fire retardant. After years of regular pruning, plants become more manageable and less costly to maintain.

However, just as pruning can be good for a garden, it can also be harmful. Topping is a notorious practice that involves cutting a tree along its trunk, leading to a dramatic increase of structurally thin and weak branches. Thinning, although usually beneficial, can increase the amount of wind breakage if too much is taken out at one time. Pruning out of season also increases fuel. Insects and diseases can infest a plant if it is pruned while its seasonal defenses are dormant.

Limbing-up is another practice that can be harmful to plants. Limbing-up involves removing the lower branches of large shrubs and trees. This highly recommended method of pruning helps keep a ground fire out of a plant's canopy. However, this is a poor practice for young plants. A young tree that has been limbed-up will focus its energy on its uppermost branches. This uneven use of energy will create more foliage at the top of the tree. Without its lower branches, a tree's trunk will not increase in diameter as rapidly. These two effects of limbing-up will eventually create a tree that is called a kite, which is prone to breaking and toppling over in strong winds.

Ivy is consuming this oak. Vines such as these can steal nutrients from the soil, raise the relative humidity (which oaks dislike), restrict a tree's growth to its outermost branches, and girdle its limbs. If the ivy is not removed, this oak will prematurely die.

Pruning Priorities

Just as a garden has pruning priorities, so do individual plants. The list that follows makes the most of time and is prioritized for fire safety.

The continual removal of the three D's—dead, damaged, and diseased wood—is the single most important task in a garden. These weak and susceptible parts of a plant should either be cut back to the trunk or to a healthy section of its branch where it can heal.

Vines, closely grown shrubs, shredding bark, and host plants, like mistletoe, should be pruned back or removed from any other large plant. Ivy and other aggressive vines should be removed from trees and shrubs.

Any branch that weakens a plant's structural integrity should be removed. Branches that cross each other or through the middle of a plant create structurally dependent growth. Crossing limbs also create wounds, as the branches rub up against each other in winds.

Both suckers, which grow from below a plant's crown, and watersprouts, which grow along a plant's trunk and limbs, should be removed. They consume nutrients that should be feeding the rest of tree, and they are structur-

ally weak. This growth is encouraged by out-of-season pruning and suddenly new conditions, such as an increase in sun, water, or nutrients. These growths are easy to spot and remove; prune back to the trunk.

Pruning Tips

Caution should be exercised when removing too much of a large plant at one time. When branches grow into each other, they become dependent and thinner. Wind and storm damage are common after heavy pruning. No more than 30 percent of a plant should be removed in one season. After allowing a plant to harden up to the new conditions, you can prune it again.

A plant that demands a lot of pruning is the wrong plant for its location. A high-maintenance plant is either too big and needs to be constantly controlled, or it is ill suited to its environment and produces a lot of unwanted wood. Remove a plant that demands a lot of pruning before the costs continue to escalate.

Pruning should be approached as a surgical procedure. Precision, timing, and technique will affect a plant's health. Below are practical tips that will help make any procedure more successful:

- **Always begin with sharp tools. A clean cut will heal much faster.**
- **Never cut beyond the last growing node on a branch, unless the cut is being made at the trunk.**
- **Always cut down into a branch.**
- **Large limbs should be taken down by three cuts, to avoid having the branch rip off. First, cut underneath the branch, several inches past its union with the trunk. Second, cut above and 1 inch farther out from the bottom cut, slowly dropping the branch. Lastly, cut the stub back to the trunk.**
- **Avoid leaving branch stubs longer than 1 to 2 inches on a trunk, but never cut the branch stubs completely flush with the trunk.**
- **Always clean and disinfect shears and saws after pruning a diseased plant. A diluted solution of bleach and water (1:25) or pure alcohol will disinfect a blade.**

Pruning Calendar

The pruning calendar below covers only those large shrubs and trees that are highly flammable. For more information on the critical aspect of timing, contact a tree company or the county U.C. Agricultural Extension office.

As a general rule, plants that bloom in summer should be pruned in spring. Plants that bloom in spring should be pruned during or immediately after flowering. Pruning at the height of the fire season is ill advised for most plants.

	Jan.	Feb.	Mar.	April	May	June	July	Aug.	Sept.	Oct.	Nov.	Dec.
Conifers			■	■	■							
California Bay and Eucalyptus					■	■	■					
Alder, Arbutus, Buckeye, Manzanita			■	■								
Berries, Buckwheat, Cotoneaster, Coyote Brush, Ivy, Oleander, Pepper Tree, Plumbago, Prunus, Rockrose		■	■	■								
Cottonwood, Maple, Poplar, Sweet Gum, Sycamore, Willow	■									■	■	■
Acacia, Cherry, Lilac, Quince			■	■	■							
Deciduous Oak			■	■	■							
Evergreen Oak						■	■					

Hiring an Arborist

Regular tree and shrub care is paramount to firescaping. However, hanging in a tree with a chainsaw is dangerous, and many individuals choose to hire arborists to prune their vegetation. As with any contractor, finding a good arborist requires knowing what to shop for.

Before interviewing arborists, you should know that tree work is expensive. The amount of insurance and type of equipment needed is the reason for the seemingly high costs. Added to the fixed costs is labor. Naturally, the more difficult a tree is to prune or remove, the higher the labor costs. Trees that are close to houses or power lines, or trees that are difficult to access (for instance, because they grow on a slope) greatly increase the costs. Also, expect to give a 10 percent or $1,000 deposit to the contractor. Lastly, a company that provides a good service, at a good value, will be busy. Try to be flexible when negotiating the start and completion dates.

Begin by asking friends and neighbors about contractors they have worked with and liked. The goal is to find three companies that are willing to come out and provide a consultation and quote. Below are the criteria used when working with the representatives from the tree companies:

Insurance

Unfortunately, a homeowner can be liable for damage or injury if a contractor is uninsured. The three important insurance certificates to ask for are liability insurance, worker's compensation, and a bond from the state for $7,500. If their claim of insurance is the slightest bit questionable, you can ask that their insurance carrier mail you a copy of the certificate.

Licensing

The fact that a company has been working in a neighborhood for a long time has little relation to the people they hire. Always ask about the experience of the individuals performing the work. The person giving the advice and quote should be a Certified Arborist. The daring individual actually doing the work should be a Certified Tree Worker, or have at least three years of experience.

References

Contractors should have references available during the initial consultation. At least one reference from each contractor should be called. Ask these references about the dependability of a company: Did they keep their word, were they timely, what was the attitude of their staff, and what kind of condition was their equipment in?

Get It in Writing

Like any negotiated agreement, get all the details in writing. The start time, the completion date, and all the work that is to be performed should be in writing. Verbal agreements lead to unmet expectations and disappointment. Lastly, never sign a contract until all of the terms are fully understood.

Chapter 10

Controlling Erosion After a Fire

As is often the case in California, one disaster begat another. On December 25, 2003, a 20-foot-high wall of mud roared through a youth camp in Waterman Canyon, San Bernardino County. Fifteen people died. The slide happened just two months after wildfires devoured the surrounding hills. Just before the slide, 3.5 inches of rain fell, causing a flash-flood warning for the camp, which was located at the base of a steep canyon that rose 1,000 to 2,000 feet above it. Maybe the campers never stood a chance, but they should have at least been aware of the risks.

The chances of erosion leap by as much as 200 percent after a hot fire. Fires eliminate canopies and clear plant litter, exposing now-barren landscapes to all environmental forces. Wind and water gain leverage when there is nothing to slow or stop them.

This chapter is first aid for a landscape. There is a test that helps diagnose the seriousness of the problem, and there are a multitude of remedies that help slow erosion for all degrees of risk. This chapter also provides long-term care suggestions, because the chances of erosion remain high four to five years following a fire. However, these recommendations are only for near-term emergency management. Once the landscape has been stabilized, it is time to jump back to the design chapters and create a landscape that can not only hold the hill, but weather the next fire as well.

The Difference Between Topsoil Loss and Landslides

Erosion is the separation and transportation of soil particles. The erosion test that follows gauges a slope's likelihood of water runoff and topsoil loss, but not of landslides. Water runoff and topsoil loss are different from soil slips and landslides, and the distinctions are important when it comes to controlling erosion. Soil particles can be moved by a variety of forces, such as water, wind, animal activity, and gravity.

Water runoff and topsoil loss are similar because they both occur on top of the land, or at least within the first several inches. Although wind is a strong force, water runoff is the leading cause of topsoil loss in the hillside communities. Excess runoff leads to a variety of environmental problems, such as decreased soil fertility, rill creation, valley infill, and degradation of fisheries. The mud that hit the youth camp in San Bernardino was in fact a product of runoff.

While the likelihood of soil slips and landslides can be calculated, these mass movements of soil, mud, and rocks occur suddenly. Slides typically occur when varying types of soils meet and separate. Gravity pulls soil and mud down a hill when either lubrication or liquefaction occurs. Lubrication is when water acts as a lubricant between different soil types, causing the top layer of soil to slip away. Liquefaction occurs when a soil becomes so saturated with water that it seemingly liquefies and gushes down a hill. The likelihood of all types of erosion increases as a soil reaches its saturation point.

Slope Failure

Slope failure implies landslides and soil slips, but not runoff. While much harder to predict than runoff because the biggest indicators lay underground, slope failure is obviously linked to the percent of slope. If your slope falls into the "most likely" category, call an expert for a second opinion and remedies.

Likelihood of Slope Failure

0–16% and 229% or more	=	Not likely
17–34% and 101–228%	=	Low likelihood
35–51%	=	Likely
52–100%	=	Most likely

Not all soil slips and landslides are predictable, but there are indicators of potential problems:

- **Slopes 50 percent or greater are prone to slides; hills between 35 percent and 50 percent are likely to slide.**
- **History is good indicator; if the site has a history of slides, then a slide may occur again.**
- **An abrupt change in a slope's steepness indicates a prior slide.**
- **An abrupt change in the plant cover may indicate a prior slide, too.**
- **A structure showing signs of pressure, such as cracks, signals soil instability.**

- **Trees and posts may lean in direction of a potential slide.**
- **Cracks in the soil that run, more or less, across a slope also indicate soil disruptions.**
- **Water bubbles and/or seeps to the surface of a hill.**
- **Watering-requiring plants, such as alder, rush, ferns or ivy, in the midst of drought adapted plants, indicate surfacing water.**
- **A landscape with an unengineered cut or fill can be prone to slides.**
- **Slopes with any of the characteristics above should be examined by a registered geotechnical engineer as soon as possible.**

Erosion Test

It is possible to estimate the chance of water runoff and topsoil loss by reviewing the following six factors: the steepness of a slope, the amount of rain, the type of vegetation burned, the site's soil type, the amount of activity by animals and humans, and the severity of the fire.

There are two assumptions about risk in the erosion test that follows. First, it assumes a heavy autumn rain, the most dangerous type of rain for a recently burned landscape. Second, it assumes that the fire was hotter than normal, killing plants and seeds that normally would have

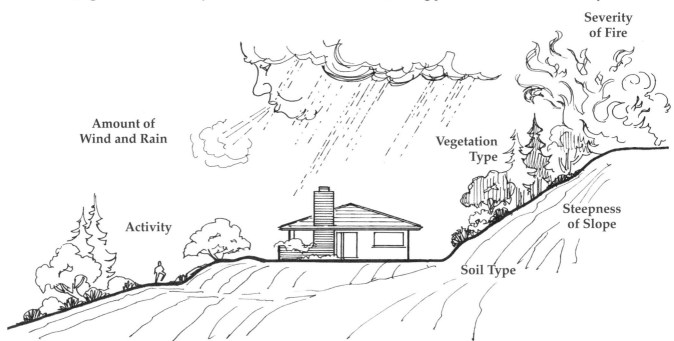

The likelihood of water runoff and topsoil loss is influenced by six measurable factors, which are highlighted in the illustration above.

sprouted and helped control erosion. These two assumptions are made because predicting rain and gauging fire severity are difficult, at best. Given these two assumptions, go through the list of contributing factors, select the line that best describes your landscape, and then add up the points. The tallied score corresponds to an approximate level of risk.

The erosion test provides indicators to the likelihood of erosion, but it cannot give accurate data. If you need accurate data for erosion risk, consult a local Certified Professional Soil Erosion and Sediment Control Specialist. Also, different parts of a landscape will score differently. Always prioritize work around the highest risk areas.

This test was developed with the help of Cagwin and Dorward, a landscape architect and engineering firm in San Rafael, California. It is a slightly modified version of the Universal Soil Loss Equation, a nationwide standard developed for farmers, with the effects of fire woven in.

Slope

A slope's degree of incline has the greatest influence on its chance of producing erosion. Water, wind, and gravity all have greater impact on steeper slopes. The incline and length of a slope are two measurable factors that most affect the chances of water runoff and topsoil loss. As a general rule, when the slope's degree and length double, the chances of erosion also double. For example, a 100-foot slope has twice the erosion likelihood of a 50-foot slope.

Although slopes have a high potential for erosion, flat ground is also susceptible to water runoff and topsoil loss. Scorched and bare landscapes quickly can become compacted and nutrient deficient. When a flat surface is wet and reaches its water saturation point, the ground will begin to puddle, filling a soil's pores with tiny particles, slowing water absorption rates even more. When water absorption decreases, water runoff, sheeting, and topsoil loss increases.

Steepness of Slope

0–16%	1 point
17–34%	2 points
35–51%	4 points
52% and higher	8 points

Length of Slope

0–25 feet	1 point
26–50 feet	2 points
51–100 feet	4 points
101–200 feet	8 points

Slope Calculation

To get the percent of a slope is easy and requires only a stake, a string, and a 4-foot-long board. Pin one end of the string to the hill, loop the other end around the top of the board, and then walk downhill. When the string is taunt and level, as illustrated in figure 1, measure the string from the hill to the top of the board. The run of the slope is the length of string. The rise of the slope is the distance between the ground and where the string attaches to the board. The percent of a slope is the rise divided by the run, then rounded to the nearest number and multiplied by 100.

The degree of a slope, which is different from the percent, is the angle between the run of a slope and the actual ground. Figure 2 shows the approximate equivalencies for ratio, percent grade, and degree. Because the ratio and percent are horizontal to vertical, and degrees are circular, calculations may vary. An engineer's calculator can convert a percent of a slope to its degree by calculating the inverse tangent of the percent.

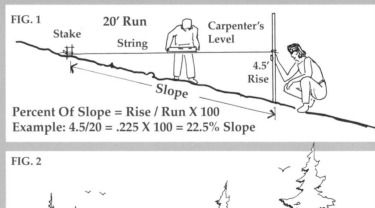

FIG. 1

20′ Run — Stake — String — Carpenter's Level — 4.5′ Rise — Slope

Percent Of Slope = Rise / Run X 100
Example: 4.5/20 = .225 X 100 = 22.5% Slope

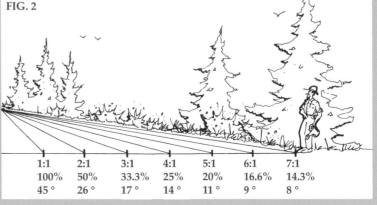

FIG. 2

1:1	2:1	3:1	4:1	5:1	6:1	7:1
100%	50%	33.3%	25%	20%	16.6%	14.3%
45°	26°	17°	14°	11°	9°	8°

Rain

How a burned landscape reacts to storms and rain depends on the amount of time between the fire and the first rain, the amount of recovery by the landscape, the amount of debris littering the landscape, and the rain's intensity and duration. A heavy autumn and winter downpour should always be planned on when testing a landscape's chances of erosion.

- **Late autumn sprinkle with light to moderate storms throughout season.**   **1 point**
- **Late autumn sprinkle with heavy winter downpour.**   **2 points**
- **No autumn rain and heavy winter downpour.**   **4 points**
- **Heavy early autumn rain and winter downpour.**   **6 points**

Type and Density of Plants Burned

This gauge is a forest-vs.-grasslands comparison. The type and density of the late landscape possess three measurable characteristics: the time to the first signs of recovery; the amount of debris littering the landscape; and the dead or injured plants' ability to hold the soils together, which is related to the rooting depth.

More often than not, the first signs of recovery come from one of the hundreds of shrubs that are able to resprout after a fire. Along the coast and in canyons, ferns and perennial grasses will resprout within days of a fire. Encouraging this growth is important because it blankets and protects the ground. Also, as these plants grow, they pull moisture from the soil, preparing the ground for the winter onslaught.

Fire-stimulated seeds and cones, such as legumes, ceanothus, and Bishop pine, are the next to show signs of recovery. Because competition has been thinned, these seeds now enjoy sufficient sunlight and full soil contact. If the fall rains are steady and light, and browsing animals minimal, these plants stand a good chance of surviving.

A wildfire in a forest leaves a much different trail than it does in grasslands or coastal scrub. Ash and burned branches lie scattered everywhere in a forest. These remains slow water. They also recharge the soil with vital minerals. As seen in some of the interior foothills, not much is left after a fire passes through the grasslands; as happens in scrub communities, winds may sweep away what little debris there is.

Not only do deep-rooting plants resprout more quickly after a fire, they also help hold the many different layers of soil together. Soil slips and landscapes are more common after fires, and low rooting depths are partially responsible. A live plant, one with deep and growing roots, is more apt to withstand the pressures of soil and gravity than a dead and decaying plant. Use the descriptions below to identify the type of landscape burned:

- **Densely forested landscape. Trees have understory shrubs and possibly ground covers growing below them.**   **1 point**
- **Landscape with scattered trees and no understory shrubs, or a landscape with only shrubs and ground covers (e.g., oak woodland and coastal sage plant communities).**   **2 points**
- **Grassy landscape with scattered perennials.**   **3 points**
- **Tough and difficult growing environments. Plants are shallow rooted, sprawling, and sparsely planted; they live in harsh and hot environments.**   **4 points**

Type of Soil

The structure, density, and size of a soil's particles influence its likelihood of erosion. Clay soils are the least erodible because of their small particles and greater density. Silt soils are moderately erodible. And although sand and gravel soils are highly erodible, because their size makes them easy to dislodge, these particles are merely rearranged and do not create the sedimentation problems that the other two soil types do. Compacted soils, which tend to be clay, produce much more runoff because of their low water-absorption rates. Water running off compacted soils carries a lot of clay and silt to and through our watersheds, slowly filling them. The ideal soil quickly absorbs water, storing some of it while letting the rest past the vegetation's root zone. A description of soil types and how to tell them apart is provided in Chapter 8.

- **Soil dominant in clay, with silt, sand, and organic matter mixed in it.** **1 point**
- **Sandy soil mixed with silt and organic matter.** **2 points**
- **Clay soil with little or no organic matter.** **3 points**
- **Sandy soil with little or no organic material. Loose and gravely rock.** **6 points**

Amount and Type of Activity

Pre- and post-fire activity by both humans and animals has a large effect on slope stability. People can dramatically alter the power and direction of water by neglecting drainage systems, improperly clearing a landscape, and practicing poor grading techniques. Tunneling animals, such as gophers, ground squirrels, and mice, are a threat to soil stability, especially if their natural predators have been displaced and their populations are large. Even something as simple as walking across a burned landscape can increase erosion because it breaks the bonds holding the particles together; it also lowers germination rates by compressing the soil, redistributing seeds, and crushing new seedlings.

- **Animals and people walking on the site.** **1 point**
- **Storm drains and gutters clogged. Tunneling and browsing animals lack predators and their populations are large.** **3 points**
- **An area that was cleared sometime before the fire, and never replanted, allowing shallow-rooted opportunists to grow.** **4 points**
- **A barren landscape, massive cuts into a hill, and/or fill brought in on a slope.** **6 points**

Fire Intensity

A low-temperature fire can cleanse and waken a dynamic landscape. A high temperature will do just the opposite; not much survives 2,000ºF. Fire intensity affects a landscape's rate of recovery and its immediate chance of erosion.

Unfortunately, high conflagration temperatures are becoming more common as the effects of successful suppression continue to age. Unhealthy plant communities create conflagration conditions, which, in turn, sterilize the landscape. Because of their age and heat, trees and shrubs are less likely to survive these fires. The intense heat also kills the hundreds of seeds that lie within the first couple inches of soil. And of great importance to gardeners, fires also create a water-repellency layer.

A water-repellency (hydrophobic) layer is created when a fire melts the waxes and resins found in plants. As a landscape cools, these waxes form a layer just below the soil. When rain hits a repellency layer, it splashes, instead of penetrates, dislodging soil particles and sending them downhill. Although most soils lose their repellency within a year, some may stay hydrophobic for up to six years. The amount of water repellency a fire creates is related to a fire's intensity and the size of a soil's particles. Larger soil particles, like sand, will have greater water repellency. Because water may not get beyond the repellency layer, and the topsoil is already eroding, germination rates for existing and broadcasted seeds will be low. However, until an erosion-control plan is developed, do not disturb the burned landscape; the repellency will protect the soil from being blown away by wind.

A decrease in soil fertility also follows a fire. Organic matter, nitrogen, and microorganisms are consumed during a fire. Luckily, though, potassium and phosphorus, two of the three most important nutrients for plants, are increased by ash. Nitrogen, which is most needed by plants, is the nutrient most lost after a fire. In severely burned and nutrient-deficient landscapes, seedlings that cannot fixate nitrogen, like rose clover, will die before they can become established. There are no points in this part of the test.

CHAPTER 10

Approximate Level of Erosion Risk

6–13 points	=	**Moderately low**
14–20 points	=	**Medium**
21–28 points	=	**Moderately high**
29–38 points	=	**High**

Perspectives: Jerry Schad, guidebook author, physical science/astronomy instructor at San Diego Mesa College, La Mesa

There's a place I visit often in the high desert part of the Anza-Borrego Desert called Culp Valley. It's right in a belt of chaparral, below the oaks and pines of the mountains and above the desert floor. I've visited the place at least once and often two or three times a year ever since I moved to southern California in 1972. Over that time, I've witnessed the effects of, maybe, four or five fires.

I remember clearly the fire that swept the entire area in August 1975. In fact, I went out there when embers were still glowing and there were clumps of smoking yuccas and agaves. No such thing as park closures back then . . . people just headed out and tramped around to take a look. Anyway, I found it fascinating because of the starkness; the burned plants looked totally black against a clear blue sky and skeletal mountains off in the distance.

I go back to Culp Valley every year during the early fall season for weekend field trips for my astronomy students. The site is often windy, and small fires break out every few years due to careless campers. Back around early '80s, our class was visiting the Clark Lake Radio Observatory down on the desert floor in the early afternoon when we spotted distant puffs of smoke to the west, right where I judged that evening's campsite in Culp Valley to be. Sure enough, by the time we got back there, a small fire had blazed through very near where we had set up our telescopes the previous night.

Nature's regenerative power is amazing to me. After 32 years of visiting this one site, I've seen its clothing of scrub oak, sugar bush, yucca, juniper, and cholla cactus go through several cycles of apparent death and rebirth. On average, I'd say the place looks about the same . . . always changing and always the same.

Fire First Aid

Once the landscape has been tested and the areas of greater and lesser risk have been identified, the next step is deciding on remedies and developing an action plan.

A landscape's risk of erosion will influence a gardener's response. If a landscape has a high risk of erosion, several remedies will be needed. For example, a steep slope that has a moderately high risk may need a wall of sandbags at the top of a hill to channel the water away from the slope; small rocks in the naturally occurring gully to catch sediment; and a combination of carefully selected seeds and jute mesh, which will hold the topsoil in place. If, on the other hand, a landscape has a low risk of erosion, the most appropriate response is to clean the landscape, encouraging the sprouting opportunists, and planning a new, fire-retardant landscape.

Along with remedies for all types of risk, this section provides general guidelines on how to work on a recently burned landscape and which seeds to use to control erosion. All efforts to slow in erosion serve one of three major goals, called the three Ds: diverting, draining, and depowering water.

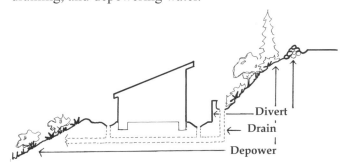

Controlling erosion means managing the three Ds: depowering, diverting, and draining water.

Guidelines for Recently Burned Landscape

A well-planned and quick response to the possibility of erosion is needed in a domestic landscape. Before starting, however, the new conditions and processes should be understood. Working on a burned landscape can cause erosion.

Clean Gutters and Drains

Drainage ditches, pipes, gutters, and small dams should be cleaned immediately after a fire. Misdirected water from poorly maintained drainage devices is a leading cause of erosion, fire or not. Expect a lot of drainage maintenance two years following a fire because of the increase of transportable debris.

Minimize Traffic

Keep all foot and equipment traffic on the burned site down to an absolute minimum. Any activity on a slope will increase the likelihood of erosion. Activity weakens a soil's bonds, dislodging soil particles. Activity on a slope may also disrupt the pattern of existing seeds, lowering germination rates. On flat ground, walking or working will compact the soil, lowering water-absorption rates. All avoidable work should be done after the threats of winter rain and erosion have passed.

Gently Clean

Debris provides obstacles to wind and water, and should not be removed until a plan of action has been developed. Once erosion work has begun, a gardener can prune the dead and injured limbs off surviving trees and shrubs.

Weeds should be encouraged to grow. Called opportunists, these weeds will help break the repellency layer, bring nutrients to a soil's surface, and help hold the hill until more desirable plants take hold. Typically annuals, some of these plants also have the ability to recharge the soil with nitrogen. Later, mowing the weeds before they go to seed will give the preferred plants a chance to grow.

Water

Watering a recently burned landscape is beneficial for a variety of reasons. Watering recharges a soil with moisture, encouraging the surviving shrubs and seeds to sprout. It helps bind the finer soil particles together, protecting a bare landscape from the wind. Gently watering after a fire also begins to break down a soil's water-repellency layer.

However, watering immediately before or during the rainy season can increase the amount of erosion a landscape creates. The ground will reach its water-saturation point more quickly if it's moist before the first rains, which will increase water runoff, topsoil loss, and the chance of soil slips. Water the injured site just enough to keep the opportunists alive, but avoid deep watering.

Seed

Seeding a landscape to control erosion is a temporary solution to the problem. If a landscape is not replanted with deeper-rooted ground covers and shrubs, the risk of soil slips and landslides will be greater in four to seven years, as the burned landscape's roots decompose and their grip on a hill weakens.

Importantly, be picky when choosing seeds. Some of the erosion mixes do indeed work, but only because they include aggressive plants. Annual ryegrass, for example, competes with desirable trees and shrubs, readily reseeds itself, and creates an abundance of flash fuels. Aggressive annuals can also migrate to native landscapes.

Protect High-Risk Areas

Slopes that have a high chance of erosion or are too steep with loose material, or areas that have already slipped, should not be planted or touched. Instead, water should be diverted away from the slope and plastic sheeting laid over the area. A soils engineer should then be called. Work on risky sites increases its instability.

Erosion Controls

The following recommendations for controlling erosion are used when the risk of water runoff, topsoil loss, and/or soil slips are likely. These recommendations are organized around the Three Ds.

Divert Water

Diversion techniques are normally used to protect vulnerable areas from sheeting water coming from streets and other properties. The first response to any injured landscape should be keeping this sheeting water off the injury. Below are a variety of the common methods for temporarily diverting water:

Boards: Typically used for depowering water, boards can divert, too. Using pretreated wood, at least 1 foot high and no thinner than 1 inch thick, run them across the top of the soil. The boards are kept in place by pounding #3 rebar 1 foot into the ground. At least a

2 percent cross-slope is needed to keep the water and mud moving along the boards. If water cannot move along the boards, the water and soil will back up, eventually saturating the soil and increasing the chances of a soil slip. Make sure that the boards always funnel the water toward a drainage system.

Diversion Ditch: A diversion ditch channels water away from structures and erosion risk areas. These ditches are trenches dug into a hill, which collect the water that flows onto a property. Diversion ditches usually channel the water to natural or artificial swales.

Dry Walls: These small rock or concrete walls are used to channel and slow water, protecting structures and roads. These walls are made from stacked concrete or rock. Dry walls are inexpensive and quickly built. While dry walls can usually be constructed with materials found on a landscape, they are not as good as sandbags, boards, and ditches for diverting water.

Plastic Sheeting: Plastic sheeting is an extreme measure and used to protect a soil's surface from rainfall. This method of erosion control is used on slopes that are likely to slide. Rolled out across a steep slope, the plastic is buried under the soil at the top of the hill and then kept in place with sandbags, heavy rocks, or pins. Importantly, once the plastic is in place, build barriers, such as sandbags or drains, to channel water away from the hazardous area.

Sandbags: A common sight after burns and in flood areas, sandbags channel water and mud away from structures and roads. Fill the bags halfway with sand, and tuck their ends under themselves. When building the wall, the bags should be staggered, with the tucked end facing the flow of water. After a row of sandbags is laid, it should be stomped on, removing the air pockets that would allow seepage later. Sandbags can also be used to hold down plastic sheeting and erosion-control matting. Sandbags are readily available and inexpensive.

Drain Water

Managing the flow of water is a science, and if a property has problems with erosion because of poor drainage, then a professional should be called. An erosion expert can calculate rates of flow, peak flow periods, and the best methods to use for drainage.

Diversion ditches are used in emergencies and are created by digging out channels across the face of a landscape. For a ditch to be effective, it must have at least a 2 percent slope. Because of the damage fast water creates, ditches with a slope of 5 percent or greater must be paved. Ditches can easily become, and cause the creation of, gullies; they are only a temporary solution to drainage problems.

Depower Water

To some degree, almost every landscape experiences runoff and topsoil loss. Removing water's ability to move things will greatly reduce the degree of loss. Friction and resistance are the characteristics to look for when selecting methods and materials to depower water. While the most commonly used devices are listed on the following pages, anything that will slow and depower water, such as concrete blocks, will work.

This dry wall was swiftly constructed, and at little cost. It will also last much longer than bales. This picture was taken one year after a fire.

In order to protect a road from excessive runoff and sediment, the owners of this burned property got creative and used broken-off branches. Anything that slows water also impedes erosion.

Used to control erosion after a fire years ago, these bales are still helping to slow water and catch sediment.

Bales: Oat, barley, wheat, and rice straw bales are used to slow water and catch sediment. These relatively inexpensive barriers are used in canyons, drainage ditches, swales, and any place where water and sediment are likely to flow. Bales are placed end to end and then staked with wood stakes or #3 rebar. Always stake them on their downhill side. The bales can be recycled into the landscape after they have lost their usefulness. Unlike the other bales, rice straw will not create a future weed problem.

Boards: By reducing the length and steepness of a slope, boards slow water and catch sediment and small rocks. Staggered along a slope, the wood should be pretreated, at least 1 foot high, about 5 feet long, and no thinner than 1 inch. The boards are kept in place by pounding #3 rebar at least 1 foot into the ground. Avoid creating a continuous line of boards across a hill; if a little water is not able to slip through, then the soil will eventually become saturated and the chances of a soil slip will increase. Do not backfill the boards.

Chain-Link Fences: These barriers are used to catch rocks and boulders from rolling into structures and roads. Metal fences are placed along the bottom of rocky slopes or at the end of gullies. Avoid using 4-by-4-inch or thinner wooden posts to anchor a fence; these posts will fracture and break when hit by a heavy rock. The uphill side of this barrier needs to be regularly cleaned to avoid a damming effect created by litter and debris; this type of depowering device is not intended to slow or stop the flow of water.

Check Dams: These barriers are used primarily in gullies and are designed to stop or slow plant material, rocks, debris, and sediment from flooding through narrow crevices. Depending on the size of the gully,

dams can either be constructed like boards, using wood and rebar, or like chain-link fences, with the posts buried 2 feet into the ground.

Dry Walls: These small rock or concrete walls are also used in diverting water. They're inexpensive to build and can be erected quickly.

Fiber Roles: Made from straw, rice hulls, and even coconut waste, these organic rolls lay across the face of slopes. The roll is laid in a trench, which is 4 inches deep and as wide as the roll, and stabled every 4 feet, with pins or stakes. At a minimum, rolls are laid every 10 feet on slopes of 50 percent or greater, 15 feet apart on 25 percent or greater, and 20 feet apart for gentler slopes. It is important to stake the ends facing uphill.

Matting: Used to slow water runoff and topsoil loss, matting is widely prescribed. It can be organic or inorganic, and is rolled out over a hill after seeding and/or mulching. Jute mesh, thin wood lattice, plastic netting, and even chain-link fencing are used as matting. Store-bought pins, thick wire coat hangers, or drip-irrigation tubing staples are used to pin the matting down.

In an effort to stop tainted water from entering the community drainage systems, this property's owners employed a variety of erosion-controlling methods. Sandbags, fiber rolls, and jute matting ensure that little or no water flows off the landscape.

Mulch: The uses for mulch are as varied as its many types. Mulch is used to protect a soil's surface from the impact of water. On slopes, mulch that is not held down with matting may have to be punched into the soil. Punching mulch into the soil by sticking it with a pitchfork helps to keep it from being blown or washed away. Although straw and recently chipped vegetation are less-expensive mulches, they initially rob the soil of nitrogen, which makes them less than ideal for protecting broadcasted seeds.

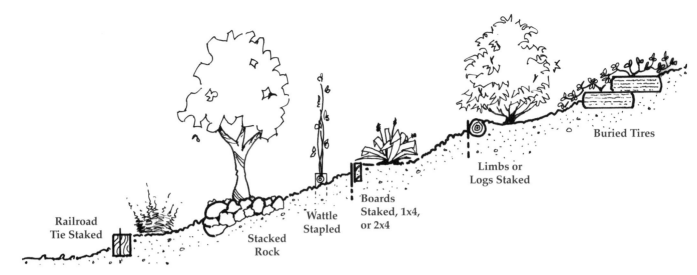

Railroad
Tie Staked

Stacked
Rock

Wattle
Stapled

Boards
Staked, 1x4,
or 2x4

Limbs or
Logs Staked

Buried Tires

The illustration above shows some of the many ways to create planting pads on a slope. Pads make planting easier and water retention more likely. The smaller the plant, the easier it is to dig into a slope. New plants should be no bigger than 1 gallon, while 4-inch and flat starts are preferred. It is important to backfill the plant with the surrounding soil that has been loosened; do not mix in soil amendments. If the plant needs the foreign imports, it is the wrong plant for that hill. Driving stakes into a rocky slope is not always advised, as it might cause soil separation.

According to the property owners, this naturally occurring gully had caused years of problems. After they filled the gully with riprap, the water and mudflows stopped.

Planting: Most of the remedies included in this chapter provide a temporary fix. Planting, on the other hand, will have a large impact on a landscape's ability to slow erosion and protect a structure from fire for many years to come. Care and consideration should be given. Chapters 4, 5, and 7 cover this topic well. However, do not delay for long; the new plants will have to establish hill-holding roots before the burned and dead plants lose their grip.

Riprap: Rock that is used to slow or manage water is called riprap. It can be almost any size and include broken concrete. It can be used to line ditches and swales, make check dams, blanket a slope, and help protect shores from wave erosion. Riprap is not recommended on slopes greater than 33 percent.

Seeds: The preferred type of seeds and instructions on sowing them are provided in the next section.

Wattle: Because of their aggressive roots, willows are widely used to control erosion along California's freshwater corridors. A wattle is a tightly wrapped bundle of long willow twigs. These bundles are placed in trenches no deeper than 4 inches and run across the face of a slope.

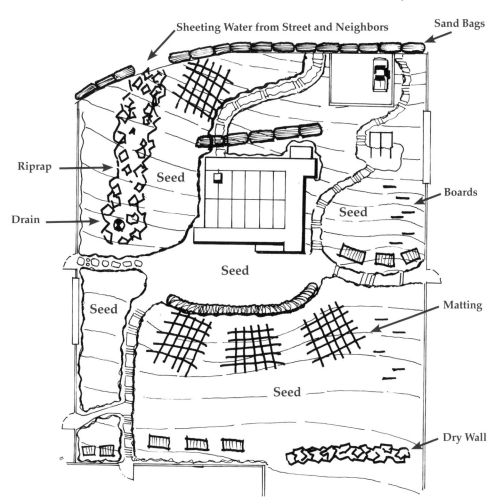

Sheeting Water from Street and Neighbors

Sand Bags

Riprap

Seed

Drain

Seed

Boards

Seed

Seed

Seed

Matting

Seed

Dry Wall

The property above employs a variety of methods to control erosion. Sandbags have been placed around the uphill side of the house to divert water coming in from the street and neighbors' properties. The riprap on the left side will guide and slow the water. The boards placed in the gully on the right side will slow the water, allowing the soil particles to drop. The shoulders along the top of the property and the downhill side of house have been shored up with a combination of seeds and matting, protecting the steep and bare ground. The dry wall below the house will slow and direct water away from the neighbor's property. Bales have been placed on the uphill side of paths. The rest of the garden has been seeded with a wildflower mix to provide color until the landscape is replanted.

Seeding a Burned Landscape

Seeding is used to depower the water, thus decreasing water runoff and topsoil loss. Seeding is preferred to planting because an area can be quickly covered in vegetation with little activity and cost. While it may not be needed throughout a landscape, broadcasting over barren ground exposed to wind and rain is a good idea. Sometimes, seeding can do more harm than good, as in native and many natural landscapes. In these landscapes, it is better to encourage the surviving trees, shrubs, and seeds. The naturally occurring plants support a much larger biological community and are probably better at holding the hill.

Water means recovery, and a landscape with this valuable resource will recover more quickly. The processes of revegetation can begin immediately. A hose-end irrigation system, discussed in Chapter 8, is a quick method for getting water to a landscape. The number of seeds a landscape can support is much larger with supplemental water.

Landscapes without supplemental water must wait for the rain to inspire the seeds within the soil. In October, the start of the rainy season, erosion-controlling seeds must be ready. The selected seeds should be aggressive and quick growing. The amount of time between the seeding and first rains affects germination rates. The longer the delay, the greater the chance the seeds will be disturbed by birds, foot traffic, and wind. Seeds require between 6 and 14 days of moist soil to sprout. If the time between sowing the seeds and the first rain is longer than a month, the area will have to be seeded again. Matting is laid over a seeded area if the risk of erosion is likely.

Once the seeds have taken root and the topsoil is covered by vegetation, planting can begin. For a landscape with supplemental water, planting can usually begin in spring. A landscape without supplemental water may have to wait until the following rainy season. It is important to avoid planting until the hill is stabilized or the threat of rain is over.

CHAPTER 10

The type of seeds sown over a recently burned landscape depends on the site's risk of erosion and whether it has irrigation water. All seeds listed below for irrigated and non-irrigated landscapes have been evaluated on four aspects of growth: whether they need supplemental water; whether they are annuals or perennials; their ability to slow erosion; and their relative competitiveness and ability to restrain other plants' growth.

Seeds for Irrigated Landscapes

Dimorphopheca spp. (African daisy): Annual. Helps low-risk erosion areas. Low competitiveness. Used for temporary color.

Festuca spp. (fescue): Perennial. Helps low to moderate risk. Competitiveness varies with species. Excellent all-purpose grasses.

Gazania spp.: Perennial. Helps low to moderate risk. Low competitiveness. Colorful and widely used on sunny slopes.

Lobularia maritima (sweet alyssum): Annual. Helps low risk. Low competitiveness. Used in mixes to give color until other plants become established.

Osteospermum fruticosum (freeway daisy): Perennial. Helps low to moderate risk. Moderately competitive. Common on sunny slopes with only a light freeze. Closely related to the African daisy

Trifolium fragiferium (O'Conner's strawberry clover): Perennial. Helps low to moderately high risk. Moderately competitive. This deep-rooting cover is tough and tolerates heat.

Seeds for Non-irrigated Landscapes

The seeds recommended below can be used on irrigated landscapes as well:

Agropyron spp. (wheatgrass): Perennial. Helps low to moderate risk. Moderately competitive. Good grasses for Sierra Nevada and other mountainous regions because they grow in the cold, heat, and semi-alkaline soils.

Bromus carinatus (California brome): Perennial. Helps low to moderate risk. Moderately competitive. A native used on burned but fertile sites.

Bromus mollis (Blando brome): Annual. Helps moderate to moderately high risk. Moderately competitive. Excellent for recently disturbed areas below 4,000 feet.

Bromus rubens L. (Panoche red brome): Annual. Helps moderate to moderately high risk. Moderately/highly competitive. One of the most drought-tolerant grasses. Excellent for disturbed areas with low fertility. Can become a weed.

Elymus glaucus (blue wild rye): Perennial. Helps low to moderate risk. Moderately competitive. A native used for habitat restoration, there are other varieties better adapted to high elevations. It is slow to germinate and grow.

Festuca rubra (red fescue): Perennial. Helps low risk. Low competitiveness. Good fescue along coast below 4,000 feet. This native is slow growing and bunches when mature.

Hordeum brachyantherum (meadow barley): Perennial. Helps moderate risk. Low to moderate competitiveness (depending on amount of water). This native grass will not choke other perennials and shrubs.

Hordeum vulgare (annual barley): Annual. Helps moderate to moderately high risk. Moderately competitive. Not as aggressive as annual ryegrass.

Lolium multiflorum (annual ryegrass): Annual. Helps moderately high risk. Very competitive. The most commonly used annual in high-risk areas because it requires less moisture to germinate (which means it's quick) and readily reseeds itself. However, this cool-season annual is aggressive and will choke out deeper-rooted perennials and shrubs, becoming a weed and flash fuel in late summer. Some subspecies possess less aggressive characteristics.

Trifolium hirtum (rose clover, Hykon rose clover): Annual. Helps low to moderately high risk. Moderately competitive. Excellent on sterile slopes because of its ability to capture atmospheric nitrogen and make it useable, this plant helps replace the nutrient most lost in a fire. To fixate nitrogen, the clover has a symbiotic relationship with the nitrifying rhizobia bacteria. It is important to make sure the bacteria (innoculum) is added to the seeds before broadcasting.

Vulpia myuros (Zorro annual fescue): Annual. Helps moderate to moderately high risk. Moderately competitive. Excellent native seed for native areas that need quick protection. Does not choke struggling perennials and shrubs. May be sold commercially as *Festuca megulara*.

Wildflower mixes: Annual and perennial. Helps low to moderate risk. Low to moderate competitiveness. Mixes may include *Achillea* spp. (yarrow), *Consolida ajacis* (larkspur), *Eschscholzia californica* (California poppy), *Gaillardia* spp. (blanket flower), *Linum grandiflorium* (scarlet flax), *Lupinus* spp. (lupine), *Myosotis* spp. (forget-me-not), *Nemophilia menziesii* (baby blue eyes), *Oenothera* spp. (evening primrose), *Rudbeckia hirta* (black-eyed Susan), and *Sisyrinchium bellum* (blue-eyed grass).

Hydroseeding, which is a blend of seed and mulch glued together, has higher germination rates than broadcasting by hand. Sprayed from a truck with a long hose, hydroseeding is quick, effective, but expensive. The type of seeds in a hydroseeding mix can be tailored to a specific landscape.

Sowing Seeds

Broadcasting seeds should only be done after all other devices to divert and drain water have been installed. At the very least, water should be diverted away from the area to be seeded. The rate of success for seeds hinges on a variety of factors, including the amount of moisture, amount of topsoil, temperature, and type of wildlife, such as birds and deer. Follow the steps below to seed a recently burned landscape:

Water: Watering several days prior to seeding will help break the water-repellency layer and begin to recharge the soil. Ideally, the soil should be slightly moist and crumbly when seeding. If soil sticks to the bottom of boots, it is too wet to seed. Turn the water off at the first signs of runoff.

Rake: Raking the ground before seeding has several benefits: It breaks the water-repellency layer, removes the larger debris that would inhibit germination, and mixes the ash into the soil. A grass rake is perfect for this task and should turn the first inch of the soil. As a slope gets steeper, the raking should get gentler.

Broadcast: If a site has irrigation water, broadcasting can start immediately. If a site has no water, seeding should begin a week prior to the first rain, which in California can be anywhere between the first two weeks in October to December. On average, it takes 6 to 14 days of moist soil for seeds to sprout.

Broadcasting can be done with a seed spreader, granular fertilizer applicator, or by hand. A big, secondhand purse is perfect to use as a seed bag. Always place more seed uphill and in areas exposed to wind. Scarecrows, noisemakers, or reflective ribbons will help deter birds from eating the seeds, which is important in areas without irrigation.

Mulch: Mulching a seeded landscape will help protect the seeds, conserve water, and slow the erosion. The mulch should be thin and light, comprised of hay, straw, or humus. Heavy and thick mulches reduce the number of seedlings. If the burned vegetation left a lot of debris, mulching may not be necessary.

Tapping: Gently tapping the ground after seeding increases germination rates. It pushes the seeds into the ground, enveloping them in soil; prevents the seeds and mulch from being blown away; and helps protect seeds from predators. Tapping is done by lightly walking or pushing an empty lawn roller over the seeded area. As a slope levels out, the tapping should be lighter.

Fertilize: Nitrogen, phosphorus, and potassium are the main nutrients required by growing plants. Nitrogen is greatly reduced after a fire. Ash, however, adds plenty of phosphorus and potassium. High doses of nitrogen are not recommended though, because they promote too much growth too quickly. Liquid fertilizers can be used on landscapes with irrigation water, but should only be used after the first signs of growth. A slow-release granular fertilizer, like ammonium nitrate, can be used on landscapes without irrigation water and should be applied only after the first rain. Fertilizers are not recommended in the native and natural landscapes that receive no maintenance.

Water Again: A watering schedule can now begin. Because only the top 2 inches need to be moist, watering should be light and gentle. On slopes, watering several times a day, for only brief intervals, may be required. *Do not overwater.* Depending on the degree of slope, a landscape will either become compacted or produce runoff if it is too wet before the rains come.

CHAPTER 10

After the Threat of Erosion Passes

Unfortunate but true—a community that just has weathered a fire will have a moderately high chance for another. The potential for fire rests with fuel and heat.

The late summer/early fall that follows a fire can be particularly dangerous. Charred and dead trees, stumps, branches, and garden features have been kiln-dried and are easily reignitable. If seeds were used to control erosion in areas with no irrigation, most of these plants will either be dead or dormant—creating an abundance of flash fuels. Rebuilding puts a lot of ignitable fuels on a landscape, too, because piles of dried lumber usually surround open and unprotected structures.

The owners of this property have decided to leave this one dead tree standing, perhaps as a somber reminder. They lost their home a year earlier and are building on the same footprint. If they can maintain the open, parklike landscape they have now, they should not have to rebuild after the next fire.

After the threat of erosion passes, managing the landscape for the next fire season moves up in priority. Dead and dying vegetation should be pruned and removed. Limbs or stumps larger than 9 inches in diameter can be left on a landscape if they have contact with the soil, which keeps them moist and speeds decomposition. Grasses and unwanted weeds must be mowed to five inches around structures and roads. Building materials and scraps should be kept from woodland fuels. These piles should also be kept neat. It is also important to take the time to remove unwanted plants. Acacia, broom, mustard, pampas grass, bramble, and honeysuckle are just a few of the flammable invaders that are easy to control after a fire.

The dead yet still-standing trees on a landscape pose another problem—toppling over. Winter winds wreak havoc on a landscape weakened by fire. Unfortunately,

The pines and oaks left standing after this fire add a lot of flammable fuel to the already fire-prone landscape. In a year these dead trees will be tinderbox dry, making them relatively easy to reignite. The costs to clean this landscape will be high.

removing trees is expensive. Some communities have negotiated with timber companies to reduce the costs. A dead tree is less dangerous if it is lying down; trees within 100 feet of a structure or road should at least be cut down and stripped of its limbs.

If a community has experienced a fire, they have had one before and will most likely have another. History has proven that Californians cannot stop fire, but only delay it (with conflagration consequences). Protecting a property against fire, rather than attempting to prevent fire, is the best way to live more peacefully with nature.

Almost a year after a fire, this small community is quick to recover and rebuild. However, the potential for another devastating fire still exists. Dead, bone-dry trees create a fire pathway to the structure and trash pile. This new house is in its most vulnerable state.

Further Information

What to Do During a Fire

It is common to see individuals standing with a hose, watering their garden or roof during a wildfire. There are, however, many other chores that precede watering with a hose. In some cases, watering a roof is a poor use of time. Below are prioritized tasks for anyone defending their home against a wildfire. In most situations, firefighters will ask everyone to leave the fire area. If they ask, do not hesitate to go.

Protect Yourself and Others

Safely get all members and pets out of the house and away from the fire area.

Get dressed for the fire. Put on wool or cotton pants, a long sleeve shirt, and a jacket. Also, grab a pair of gloves, a handkerchief, and goggles for added protection.

Move and park cars off driveways and roadways so emergency vehicles can get by.

Pack all irreplaceable items, such as photos, art, address books, bonds, stocks, birth certificates, pets, and the stuff you'll need for a couple days away from home, such as medications, toiletries, and a change of clothes. Place all of this in the car. Make sure to roll all the windows up. Leave the doors unlocked and the keys in the ignition. Even if the roads become unusable, a car is a safe place for irreplaceable items.

Fill as many containers as possible with drinking water. You'll need several bottles of water to quench your thirst and to keep the handkerchief around your face moist.

Pack valuables, such as jewelry and clothes, in weighted plastic bags and toss them into a pool or pond.

Protect the Inside of a Home

Turn off the gas at the line leading to the house.

Shut all doors and windows inside a house. Remove flammable drapes from windows. Close venetian blinds and other nonflammable window coverings. Close storm shutters. Close all attic, basement, and eave vents.

Fill sinks and bathtubs with water. Place towels or rugs next to these indoor water reserves. The water reserves and towels can be used to extinguish flames within a structure.

Turn on all the lights in a house. A smoke-filled house is difficult to see and navigate in.

Papers Needed in an Emergency

If you live in an area prone to fires, the following papers should be kept together and in a transportable case: insurance polices, deeds/home-loan papers, medical/Medicare cards, birth/death certificates, social security numbers, passports, tax returns (past three years), will/trust documents, titles to vehicles, professional licenses/certificates, medical information, bank account numbers, and household inventory.

Turn off fans and cooling systems.

Leave all doors unlocked. In the fires of 2003, one fireman was seriously injured and another died trying to get into a house that was locked.

Protect Your Pets

There are three options for pets during a wildfire: flee with the owner, stay in a safe place while the owner fights the fire, or be stranded with no help. Steps can be taken to increase the chances of survival in all three circumstances. Naturally, it is always safer for the owner and pet to flee a fire.

Make sure the animal has an identification tag.

Many emergency shelters refuse to take pets. It is important to know where you can safely drop yours off. A network of family, friends, and some hotels should be prearranged.

If you decide to fight the fire, place the pet in a familiar, safe, and secure spot, such as a car.

Carry a photo of your pet for possible identification reasons.

Grab a week's worth of food and medicine.

If for any reason you have to flee without taking your pet, then uncage or unleash it.

Protect the Outside of a Home

Remove all combustible items from under and around the house. Examples include stored newspapers, firewood, furniture, and plants that have grown up and under a house.

Place a ladder against the side of the house, creating easy access to the roof.

Sweep and clean the roof of all ignitable material.

Clean obstacles, such as patio furniture, from around the house, and put them inside the house or out in the yard.

Hook up hoses to every water faucet around the house. Attach an adjustable nozzle at the end of each hose.

Place shovels, rakes, and hoes in a visible place.

Place large, watertight cans and buckets around the house, then fill them with water. Place towels and rugs next to the water buckets. If for some reason water becomes unavailable, these wet towels will help beat out small sparks and flames.

Water combustible roofs now. To make the most of water's limited supply, stand below the roof and shoot water up into it. Unlike watering the roof from above, watering from below gets the water into the small cracks and crevices, where sparks are likely to get caught, without the excess water runoff.

Phone Problems

If in a disaster your phone does not work, try using a pay phone. These phones have a priority dial tone and may continue working during an emergency.

Glossary

check dams Objects put in a gully or swale to slow water and catch debris. The dams can be small, like rock, or large, like chain-link fencing.

clay soil Dense soil composed of the smallest particles. Also called heavy or adobe.

combustibility A term used to describe the amount of heat a plant or landscape will produce when on fire. Combustibility is related to moisture content, density, and chemical composition.

conflagration A fire that is large, destructive, and uncontrolled. Usually associated with strong winds that carry firebrands over natural and artificial barriers.

controlled burn Burning piles of debris, typically vegetation. In most residential areas these fires require a permit.

crown This term applies to the top and bottom of a plant. The entire branch structure of a plant is its top crown. Canopy is another word for the top crown. The sometimes-enlarged union where the roots meet the top structure is the root crown.

defensible space A 30-foot area around a structure that has low fuels, discontinuity of fuels, and high moisture. The defensible space is where firefighters will defend a home; also called zone 1 or the garden zone. Defensible space is just one part of the firebreak required by state law. See *firebreak*.

domestic landscape A landscape that is planned and regularly maintained. Home gardens and city parks are examples of domestic landscapes.

dormancy The annual slowing of a plant's metabolism. Dormancy is an adaptation to environmental extremes, such as drought or freeze.

drip line An imaginary line drawn in the soil, directly below the outermost branches of a tree or shrub.

dry walls Staked rock or concrete walls that are used to channel water.

emergency water The water used to combat a fire. A good water source, such as a pool, plus a pump and hoses are the basic components of an emergency watering system.

erosion The separation and transportation of soil particles by water, wind, gravity, and activity.

fiber rolls Straw, rice, and coconut waste that has been rolled and bound to create long rolls. Laid out across the face of a slope, these rolls reduce topsoil loss. They are partially buried and staked.

fire adapted Plants that have evolved to the reoccurrence of fire to the point where fire will aid in reproduction. Acquired devices include thick seed coats, nitrogen fixing, resin-protected (fire-stimulated) seeds and cones, resprouting ability, accelerated maturity, and, as in the case of the redwoods, thick bark, and copious amounts of litter. These individual adaptations can also serve other functions.

firebreak An area with little or no ignitable fuels. According to the California Department of Forestry and Fire Protection, a firebreak of not less than 100 feet must be maintained around all structures in high fire-hazard communities. A firebreak can also be a road, a driveway, a walkway, or a concrete patio. Firefighters will typically battle a blaze in a firebreak.

fire dependent A plant or ecosystem that requires fire to either aid in its reproduction and/or maintain stability.

fire ladder Any plant, or grouping of plants, that would allow a ground fire to leap into trees.

fire pathway Any grouping of plants that allows a fire to travel across a property.

fire prone A plant community that has a long, documented history of fire and of which fire may aid in the community's stability. A plant that is more prone to ignition will have high oil content, twiggy growth, a lot of deadwood, and a short life span. The coastal sage scrub plant community is considered fire prone and has many fire-prone (also called pyrophytic) plants.

fire resistant A plant's ability to resist the effects of fire. Fire-resistant plants may resprout after injury, have protective bark, and have a structure that has high ignitability but low combustibility, which minimizes injury. These plants are recommended for firescaping zones 2 and 3.

fire retardant A plant that is reluctant to burst into flames. These plants have low fuels and high moisture. Succulents, yarrow, and foxglove are some of the many fire-retardant plants. These plants are recommended for firescaping zones 1 and 2.

firescaping A style of landscape design and maintenance that protects a house and property from wildfires. Healthy, clean, and clear are the threads that tie all firescaped gardens together. The word was coined by California native Bob Perry in the early 1980s.

fire suppressed This is a politically debated term that is commonly used to describe a landscape that has adapted to the recurrence of fire, but has not had a fire for a long time.

fire weather A combination of low humidity, high temperatures, and winds. Fire weather is at its extreme during the easterlies of late summer and early autumn.

flammability A term used to describe the fire potential of a plant, house, or landscape. The fire potential of an object is based on its combustibility, ignitability, and sustainability.

flash fuel A plant fuel that is relatively easy to ignite. Natural grasses, and to a greater degree the annual varieties, are considered flash fuels.

foehn wind A dry, offshore wind. These winds are created when the atmospheric pressure over the Great Basin is greater than the pressure over the Pacific Ocean; high goes to low and the air is dried and heated as it is pushed up and over the mountains that separate these two areas. Monos, Santa Anas, and easterlies are examples of foehn winds.

fuel break See *greenbelt*.

gallons per minute (gpm) A term used to describe the flow rate of water. The gallons of water a water source will provide in a minute.

greenbelt An area that is very low in ignitable fuels. Often called a fuel break, these regularly maintained landscapes will dramatically slow a fire. Firescaping's zone 2.

high-pressure watering system Hose-end, impulse heads, and pop-ups are examples of sprinkler heads that require high pressure to water a large area. Good for large areas of plants that have identical needs.

ignitability A term used to describe the temperatures and conditions that are required to get a plant or landscape to burst into flames. Ignitability is determined by moisture content, chemical composition, and leaf size.

landslide A mass of sliding rocks, soil, and/or mud.

limbing-up The process of removing the lower limbs of mature shrubs and trees, usually to 6 feet off the ground. It lowers the chance that a ground fire will be able to leap into a shrub or tree. Limbing-up an immature plant is ill advised and will create a top-heavy plant, called a kite.

loam A soil rich in organic matter.

low-pressure watering systems Drips, soakers, misters, small sprinklers, and in-line tubing are examples of devices used to deliver water at a slow rate. Good for water conservation and catering to the unique needs of individual plants.

matting Any number of devices that are laid over the top of a slope to slow runoff and topsoil loss. Jute, lattice, and chain-link fencing are used as matting.

minimum watering depth (mwd) The top 50 percent of a plant's root zone.

native landscape A landscape where environmental forces, such as fires and floods, continue to shape the character of it and its plants. Human development is almost nonexistent, except for essential roads, power poles, and supporting structures.

natural landscape The most dangerous type of landscape. With a combination of native and introduced plants, the natural landscape is considered a hybrid. The vegetation is anything that can successfully reproduce. These landscapes can be any size.

overhang The part of a structure that juts out over a slope. Typically, overhangs are supported by stilts and include decks and the undersides of houses.

percentage of slope The rise of a slope divide by its run, then multiplied by 100.

preferred minimum watering depth (pmwd) The top 75 percent of a plant's root zone. The ideal depth that water should go to create healthy, deep-rooting plants.

prescribed fire A method of fuel reduction and, in some cases, habitat restoration. Used in native and natural landscapes. Prescribed fires are only started when a predetermined value for temperature, humidity, fuel moisture, and wind behavior are present.

rills and gullies Areas of concentrated erosion, causing an indented path for excess water and runoff. Rills are small gullies.

riprap Rock or broken concrete that is used to line swales, make check dams, or cover a slope.

root zone The depth and width of a plant's roots.

runoff Water that runs over a surface. Runoff occurs in soils that are receiving water faster than they can absorb it, eventually creating rills and enlarging gullies.

sedimentation The deposit of suspended particles of soil and/or rock by water and/or wind. This process occurs when the water and/or wind slows to the point that the weight of the particle is greater than the carrying force of the water and/or wind.

silt In terms of size, the soil particles that lie between sand and clay.

skirt A barrier that prevents heat, wind-blown sparks, and fires from getting under a structure. A skirt runs from the bottom of an overhang to the ground. Skirts are made from metal sheets or plywood.

soil slip Small, sliding movements of rocks, soil, and/or mud.

spark arrester A noncombustible and noncorrosive mesh that covers the outlets of heat and sparks. From chimneys and stovepipes to chippers and chainsaws, this simple device reduces the chance of ignition.

sustainability A term used to describe a plant or landscape's ability to keep a fire going. Sustainability is determined by the amount of fuel a plant or landscape has.

swale A drainage device that is typically cut into the land and used to channel water off a property. Swales should not exceed a 4 percent grade and can be vegetated, lined with rock, or protected with concrete.

topsoil The top layer of soil. This typically rich soil can be 1 inch or less on southwest-facing slopes and one foot or greater in northeast-facing canyons. Topsoils have more nutrients, better structure, and quicker water absorption than the lower subsoils.

transition zone The area that separates a domestic landscape from a native or natural landscape. This firescaping zone will slow the spread of a fire and act as a buffer between a domestic and natural or native landscape. Firescaping's zone 3.

understory The environment under a canopy of trees.

wildfire An uncontrolled fire.

willow wattling A tightly wrapped bundle of willow twigs. Partially buried and staked, these rolls will sprout if watered.

Helpful Websites

www.asca-consultants.org
American Society of Consulting Arborists: With many members in California, this group's website lists consultants that have five or more years of experience, and have a four-year degree in arboriculture, or a closely related discipline.

www.bewaterwise.org
This site is sponsored by the family of southern California water agencies. It offers in-depth advice on designing, installing, and maintaining a California heritage garden, which emphasizes the use of native plants. The site also provides a list of fire-resistant native plants.

www.cafirealliance.org
California Fire Alliance is an organization aimed at tying state and federal resources together. On this site is a table that lists all fire-prone cities in California and rates them on degree of risk.

www.ecosmart.gov
EcoSmart is a Web-based software program designed to evaluate the economic trade-offs between different landscape practices. The effects of various choices can be examined on fire risk and energy and water use.

www.fire.ca.gov
This state-sponsored site offers variety of suggestions on creating a fire-protected property. It also provides links to other emergency agencies and California's Fire Plan, which is the state's action guide to preventing and stopping devastating wildfires.

www.fireplan.gov
This site offers the federal government's action plan for preventing and stopping wildfires. It also provides insight into the policies of the various federal land managers in California.

www.firesafe.com
This site offers free hosting services for emergency agencies and provides links to many fire-protection agencies in California.

www.firesafecouncil.org
This is a great resource for communities wanting to establish a grass-roots educational campaign.

www.firewise.org
Get information on how to create a protected property from this site.

www.giyp.com
Green Industry Yellow Pages: Arborists, garden centers, landscape, architects, landscapers, specialty nurseries, tools, and much more can found on this site.

www.iinc.org
The Insurance Information Network in California offers tips on fire safety and fire insurance throughout the state.

www.ipm.ucdavis.edu
Integrated Pest Management is a fantastic method for reducing pesticides while controlling pests. This site is an excellent reference.

www.mofo.com/about/socalfirehelp
Southern California Wildfires Handbook: This site, from a leading law firm, offers a complete handbook with tips, references, and referrals, with an emphasis on legal issues, for the victims of the southern California's 2003 fires.

References and Selected Readings

Baptiste, Linda, *Firescape: Landscaping to Reduce Fire Hazard.* Oakland: East Bay Municipal Utility District, 1993.

Belzer, Thomas J., *Roadside Plants of Southern California.* Missoula, MT: Mountain Press Publishing Co., 1984.

Bolton, Joan, "Firescaping: Ways to Keep Your House and Garden from Going Up in Smoke." *Horticulture Magazine,* October 1991.

Brenzel, Kathleen Norris, ed., *Sunset Western Gardening Book.* Menlo Park, CA: Sunset Publishing Corp., 2001.

California Department of Forestry, *Fire Safe–Inside & Out.*

California Department of Forestry, Fire Safety Guides for Residential Development in California. 1982.

Crosby, Bill, "Our Wild Fire." *Sunset Magazine,* June 1992.

Dana, Richard Henry, Jr., *Two Years Before the Mast.* New York: Random House Publishing Group, 2001.

Dines, Nicholas, and Kyle Brown, *Landscape Architect's Portable Handbook.* New York: McGraw-Hill, 2001.

Ferris, Roxana S., *Native Shrubs of the San Francisco Bay Region.* Berkeley: University of California Press, 1966.

Farnham, Delbert S., *A Property Owner's Guide to Reducing the Wildfire Threat.* Jackson, CA: University of California Cooperative Extension, Amador County, 1992.

Fish, Peter, "Chaparral." *Sunset Magazine,* April 1994.

Graf, Michael, *Plants of the Tahoe Basin: Flowering Plants, Trees, and Ferns.* Berkeley: CNPS Press and University of California Press, 1999.

Hickman, James C., ed., *The Jepson Manual: Higher Plants of California.* Berkeley: University of California Press, 1993.

Hill, Lewis, and Sears, Elayne, *Pruning Made Easy: A Gardener's Visual Guide to When and How to Prune Everything, from Flowers to Trees.* Williamstown, MA: Storey Publishing, 1998.

Juhren, M. C., and Kenneth T. Montgomery, "Long-Term Responses of Cistus and Certain Other Introduced Shrubs on Disturbed Wildland Sites in Southern California." *Ecology,* vol. 58, no. 1, Winter 1977.

Kourik, Robert, *Drip Irrigation for Every Landscape and All Climates.* Santa Rosa, CA: Metamorphic Press, 1992.

Lang, Susan, ed., *Hillside Gardening.* Menlo Park, CA: Sunset Publishing Corp., 2002.

Libby, W. J., and K. A. Rodriques, "Revegetating the 1991 Oakland-Berkeley Hills Burn." *Fremontia* 20(1):12–18.

Maire, Richard G., *Landscape for Fire Protection.* Los Angeles: University of California, Division of Agriculture and Natural Resources.

Montgomery, Kenneth R., and P. C. Cheo, "Fire-Retardant Plants for Brush Fire Prevention in Hillside Residential Areas." *Lasca Leaves,* September 1970.

Montgomery, Kenneth R., and P. C. Cheo, "Moisture and Salt Effects on Fire Retardance in Plants." *American Journal of Botany* 56(9): 1028–1032.

Moore, Howard E., *Protecting Residences from Wildfires: A Guide for Homeowners, Lawmakers, and Planners.* Berkeley: Pacific Southwest Forest and Range Experiment Station, U.S. Forest Service, May 1981.

Northern California Chapter of the American Society of Landscape Architects, *Landscape Considerations to Reduce Fire Danger.* Fire Recovery Task Force, 1992.

Radtke, Klaus W. H., *Living More Safely in the Chaparral-Urban Interface.* Berkeley: Pacific Southwest Forest and Range Experiment Station, U.S. Forest Service, June 1983.

Perry, Bob, *Trees and Shrubs for Dry California Landscapes.* San Dimas: Land Design Publishing, 1987.

"Protecting Your Home Against Brushfire." *Sunset Magazine,* September 1985.

Rain Bird Sprinkler Manufacturing Corporation, *Landscape Irrigation Design Manual.* 2000.

Raven, Peter H., *Native Shrubs of Southern California.* Berkeley: University of California Press.

Smaus, Robert, *52 Weeks in the California Garden.* Los Angeles: Los Angeles Times Books, 1996.

Smith, Clifton, *A Flora of the Santa Barbara Region, California.* Santa Barbara: Santa Barbara Botanic Garden/Capra Press, 1998.

Svihra, Pavel, "The Oakland-Berkeley Hills Fire: Lessons for the Arborist." *Journal of Arboriculture,* September 1992.

Tanem, Bob, *Deer Resistant Plants.* San Rafael: Bob Tanem, 1993.

University of California Division of Agriculture and Natural Resources, *Pests of Landscape Tree and Shrubs: An Integrated Pest Management Guide.* Publication no. 3359, 1994.

University of Nevada–Reno Cooperative Extension, *Home Landscaping Guide for Lake Tahoe and Vicinity.* Publication no. EB-00-01.

Weeden, Norman F., Ph.D., *A Sierra Nevada Flora.* Berkeley: Wilderness Press, 1996.

FURTHER INFORMATION

PLANT INDEX

About the Author

Douglas Kent is an environmental horticulturalist and author. He started gardening in his mid-teens and quickly developed an irrevocable love for the mechanics of gardening and for California landscapes. He has written two books, *A New Era of Gardening* and *A Guide to California Natives,* and more than 50 articles, which have appeared in such publications as *Los Angeles Times, Marin Independent Journal,* and *Fine Gardening* magazine. Kent has created numerous fire-resistant landscapes, and has worked on community education campaigns with the Mill Valley Preparedness Committee and FireSafe Marin. He has an education in plant sciences and environmental policy and is currently doing research at Cal Poly Pomona. He also sails.

Acknowledgments

Casting off some 12 years ago, *Firescaping* has been quite a journey. It has sailed through meetings, gardens, and relationships, becoming richer with every encounter. A few people, especially, have helped me on this adventure.

My immediate family is by far the largest contributor: My dad, Richard, gave the project his gifted hands and hundreds of hours; my mom, Diane, housed and sponsored many fire expeditions; my stepmom, Marilyn, saved me from faltering several times; my twin, Debbie Dunne, developed the image for the business; my uncle, Gilbert Gillespie, was an enduring and sharp technical adviser; my sister, Dana, was the early editor; my brother, Dennis, helped create the graphs and tables; my newly adopted cousins, Harry, Ginger, and Joana Nieuwboer; and my dearest friends, Davin Palitz, Frank and Trinity Pellkofer, and Renee Harwood lent a hand and cheer to all the work.

However, the depth of this book, and that of my journey, comes from the incredible experts living in California. We are indeed a rich state. Thank you to the many people who provided review comments for this book. The following people have had an indelible impact: Adam Rowe is a gifted contractor from the Sierra; Pete Martin, Casey May, Jack Rosevear, and Keith Parker are all dedicated and bright government experts; Ray Moritz is one of the state's most passionate fire ecologists; Bob Cromwell, of Cagwin and Dorwood, donated many hours to erosion control; Calvin Goddard and the creative management at Sloat Nurseries added enormous value; Bob Tanem, a Bay Area radio gardening host, is an animated and insightful fan of fire safety; Dr. Tracy Williams and Alicia Borden gave gracious insights into human behavior; Jim Evans, Jessica Green, and importantly, Ellen Cavalli, have made the project shine; and lastly, the wonderful people at Wilderness Press, especially Roslyn Bullas, Laura Keresty, and Eva Dienel, who are determined to raise the anchor and launch this book to new shores.

Thank you.